T0419177

COLLECTIVE POLITICAL RATIONALITY

Amidst the polarization of contemporary politics, partisan loyalties among citizens are regarded as one contributor to political stalemate. Partisan loyalties lead Democrats and Republicans to look at the same economic information but to come to strikingly different conclusions about the state of the economy and the performance of the president in managing it. As a result, many observers argue that democratic politics would work better if citizens would shed their party loyalty and more dispassionately assess political and economic news.

In this book, Gregory E. McAvoy argues, contra this conventional wisdom, that partisanship is a necessary feature of modern politics, making it feasible for citizens to make some sense of the vast number of issues that make their way onto the political agenda. Using unique data, he shows that the biases and distortions that partisanship introduces to collective opinion are real, but despite them, collective opinion changes meaningfully in response to economic and political news. In a comparison of the public's assessment of the economy to those of economic experts, he finds a close correspondence between the two over time and argues that in modern democracies an informed public will also necessarily be partisan.

Modernizing the study of collective opinion, McAvoy's book is essential reading for scholars of American public opinion and political behavior.

Gregory E. McAvoy is Associate Professor at the University of North Carolina at Greensboro. He has published articles in the fields of public policy, American public opinion, and research methods.

"Theoretically rich and full of innovative data, *Collective Political Rationality* offers a major advance to the study of public opinion. By combining partisanship, political knowledge, issue salience, news, and elections into a single theoretical framework, Gregory McAvoy provides the most comprehensive picture of aggregate opinion ever."

Peter K. Enns, *Cornell University*

"McAvoy provides a stunning advance to the study of the dynamics of public opinion by melding the factors of information, partisanship and salience with the precise components of Bayesian analysis needed for a new path-breaking perspective."

Janet M. Box-Steffensmeier, *Ohio State University*

"The central argument of Gregory McAvoy's fine book—that the partisan loyalties that are often derided in popular commentary and academic writing actually provide the structure that makes collective public opinion sensible and rational—is both theoretically novel, meticulously supported through careful analysis, and, I am convinced, spot on."

Paul Kellstedt, *Texas A&M University*

COLLECTIVE POLITICAL RATIONALITY

Partisan Thinking and
Why It's Not All Bad

Gregory E. McAvoy

Routledge
Taylor & Francis Group

NEW YORK AND LONDON

First published 2015
by Routledge
711 Third Avenue, New York, NY 10017

and by Routledge
2 Park Square, Milton Park, Abingdon, Oxon, OX14 4RN

Routledge is an imprint of the Taylor & Francis Group, an informa business

Library of Congress Cataloging in Publication Data
McAvoy, Gregory E.
Collective political rationality : partisan thinking and why it's not
all bad / Gregory E. McAvoy.
    pages cm
Includes bibliographical references and index.
1. Party affiliation – United States. 2. Public opinion – Political
aspects – United States. 3. Political culture – United States.
4. Opposition (Political science) – United States. 5. Divided
government – United States. I. Title.
JK2271.M328 2015
306.2´60973–dc23   2014044984

ISBN: 978-1-138-88512-7 (hbk)
ISBN: 978-1-138-88513-4 (pbk)
ISBN: 978-1-315-71565-0 (ebk)

Typeset in Bembo
by HWA Text and Data Management, London

To Susan
For years filled with love and adventures, past and future

CONTENTS

List of Figures   *viii*
List of Tables   *x*
Preface   *xi*

1 Introduction   1

2 Public Opinion: Signal or Noise?   22

3 The Partisan Signal   48

4 Information Processing and Selective Attention   69

5 Shifting Regimes   92

6 The Good-Enough Public   113

Index   *131*

FIGURES

2.1   Simulated time series with varying signal-to-noise ratios, *r*   26

2.2   Signal and noise for support among Democrats for Barack Obama in the 2008 primary/Support for the government's economic policy   27

2.3   Foreign policy approval Gallup and CBS Data, 1981 to 2007   31

2.4   Signal and noise model for consumer sentiment, 1978 to 2012   32

2.5   Rating the economy, party by education (1985 to 2007)   37

2.6   Errors (RMSE) for presidential approval and economic evaluations and informed opinion, varying knowledge and partisanship   41

3.1   Rating the economy by party (1989 to 2012)   52

3.2   Gallup presidential job approval, Feb. 1961–Apr.2012   54

3.3   Gallup presidential job approval for Democrats and Republicans, Feb. 1961–Apr. 2012   55

3.4   In-party vs. out-party, Gallup presidential job approval, Mar. 1961–Apr. 2012   56

3.5   Immediate response to change of administration   58

3.6   Spending preferences from the General Social Survey for the environment, education, and crime by party (1973–2012)   62

4.1   The impact of strong and weak priors   72

4.2   Tracking poll for Republican primary, 2012   75

4.3   Conditional variance of in-party and out-party's use of unemployment in updating economic evaluations, 1990–2007   80

4.4   Kalman gain for partisan updating of unemployment and inflation on presidential approval, 1961–2013   82

4.5   Hearing unfavorable economic news index, 1989–2012   85
4.6   Time-varying effects of unemployment on news reception,
      1985–2012   86
4.7   Time-varying effects of unemployment and inflation on
      economic evaluations, 1985–2012   87
5.1   Time-varying parameters for the impact of economic conditions
      on evaluations of the economy, 1978–2012   96
5.2   Economic evaluations (consumer expectations), 1978–2012   98
5.3   Time-varying parameters for the impact of economic factors on
      presidential approval, 1961–2012   104
5.4   Presidential approval with estimated regimes, 1961–2012   106
6.1   Consumer sentiment index from Surveys of Consumers,
      Survey Reasearch Center, University of Michigan and
      forecast economic growth in GDP from the Survey of
      Economic Forecasters, 1989–2011   115

TABLES

2.1 Monthly correlations for economic evaluations between education and partisan groups, 1985–2007   38

3.1 Signal to noise ratio, in-party vs. out-party for presidential approval, 1961–2012   57

3.2 Signal-to noise-ratio, presidential approval, 1961–2012   65

4.1 Correlations among economic ratings, news reception, and economic conditions, 1989–2011   84

5.1 Hyperparameters for model for time-varying model of economic evaluations   96

5.2 Time frame for the estimated regimes from the changepoint model for economic evaluations   100

5.3 Changepoint model for economic evaluations   101

5.4 Hyperparameters for model for time-varying model of presidential approval   105

5.5 Time frame for the estimated regimes from the changepoint model for presidential approval   106

5.6 Changepoint model for presidential approval   108

6.1 Relationship between growth in real GDP and expert and public evaluations of the economy, 1989–2011   117

6.2 Relationship between growth in real GDP and expert and partisan evaluations of the economy, 1989–2011   119

PREFACE

I began this project wondering about the consequences of this highly partisan era on collective public opinion. Originally I was drawn into the narrative that partisanship was undermining collective opinion. Today the news is filled with stories about the partisan divide. "Republicans hate Obamacare"; "Democrats hate No Child Left Behind." Even stories about issues as seemingly nonpartisan as the flu and controlling the Ebola virus become partisan. "The Democrats are to blame for Ebola cases because the White House did not carefully manage the Centers for Disease Control (CDCs) preparedness plans." "Republicans are to blame because they cut funding to the CDC." The partisan rhetoric that fills the news filters down to the public, leading Democrats and Republican supporters to view these issues through a partisan lens. As I dug further into the issue of partisanship and collective opinion and gained a better understanding of the way that people rely on partisanship to understand the world, I was particularly struck by research showing that people who are highly informed about politics, the people that are supposed to be making sense of the world, are also some of the most partisan. Slowly it dawned on me that I, as a highly partisan and fairly well-informed citizen, was part of the problem. And not just me, but this profile includes nearly all of my family and friends. (And thanks to social media, I know that it fits most of their friends and family as well.)

Thinking about the thoughtful engaged citizens that I knew led me to explore the issue of partisanship in a new light and to question the standard narrative about the corrosive effects of partisanship. Surely partisanship—so enthusiastically embraced by so many—cannot be as bad as many news accounts and some academic literature suggests. Studying this issue further led me back to a reading that I had not looked at since I took a graduate seminar on political parties from Frank Sorauf at the University of Minnesota: the report by an APSA committee from the 1950s, "Toward a More Responsible Two Party System" (old even when I was in graduate school). The committee was commissioned to address the problem of weak and at times indistinguishable political parties. The committee reported back with an enthusiastic call for strong parties, ones that could send clear partisan signals to their members and enable them to form coherent policy preferences. As others have noted about this report, "be careful what you wish for" since the parties of today embody at least some of the prescriptions that the commission recommended for a strong party system. Although the analysis of the 1950s does not easily translate to the modern era, the report is refreshing at least in its embrace of party politics.

In this book, I side with the committee in stressing the contribution that parties make to collective opinion. Given the complexity and volume of issues that make it onto the political agenda, it seems naive to think that ordinary citizens could make sense of modern politics without relying on party cues. Obviously, partisanship can be taken to an extreme and we may at times have bumped up against those extremes in the modern era, but that does not negate the need for and value of parties in making sense of the world. I think that the contribution that parties make to public opinion described in this book are real and meaningful, and that the analysis is not an extended rationalization of my own partisanship. But, I will leave that for the reader to judge.

At the outset of this research project, I had the pleasure of working with two co-authors, Peter Enns and Paul Kellstedt, on several articles about partisanship and aggregate opinion and my analysis here clearly benefited from our collective thinking on this topic.

Others have contributed to this project as well. I have had many discussion about contemporary politics with my colleagues in the Political Science Department at the University of North Carolina at Greensboro and these have provided me with many "party cues" and information that have helped me, as a citizen and a scholar, to make some sense of the pressing questions in American politics today. And I'm particularly grateful to my friend and chair, Bill Crowther, whose subtle hints about the need to complete this book helped bring it to completion.

When I think back to how I thought this book would come to fruition, I am reminded of a line from the movie *Chariots of Fire* in which "victory...[would be] achieved with the effortlessness of the gods." Now, I didn't think completing the book would be easy, but I didn't think it would be this hard and require so much of other people, particularly those at home. So I will first thank my son, Ben, for his help with the citations, but also for his willingness to ask, "Dad, are you done with the book yet?" It doesn't take too many of these queries to get you on the road to finishing. And, finally, I want to thank Susan for her many contributions to the book. The first contribution is unique; I don't know of any other authors whose spouse's contribution was to be a data point in their research. But Susan was a respondent in the General Social Survey (GSS) and answered some of the questions that I used from the GSS in Chapter 3 of the book. And she also read nearly all of the book and contributed some obvious improvements (a revised title!) and many more substantive comments that are hard to detect now, but I know greatly improved the book. It is dedicated to her.

1

INTRODUCTION

When searching for political theater, it is hard to top the machinations surrounding the Affordable Care Act, passed in March 2010. Early in the debate, opponents labeled the plan as "socialized medicine" and set out to convince Americans that the president himself was a socialist. This strategy was followed by gross distortions of the bill by prominent politicians who claimed that in the finer details of the bill were provisions for "death panels"—committees that would determine whether elderly Americans and children with disabilities would be denied coverage in order to reduce health care costs. There were back room negotiations to bring fiscally conservative Democrats on board for the vote (including one notorious proposal aimed at garnering the support of Nebraska Senator Ben Nelson which became known as the "Cornhusker Kickback" [Jacobs & Skocpol 2010]).[1] The final vote on the House version of the bill was nationally televised and included what surely has to be one of the most dramatic (and unheralded) acts of political courage by a politician in recent memory—Bart Stupak's defense of the bill during debate and subsequent vote for it.[2] And the drama continued after the House passed the bill as the Senate leadership needed to use the reconciliation process in order to avoid a filibuster.

The health care debate captured the attention of much of the public, and the evolution of public opinion was recorded by public opinion polls. When asked about health care reform prior to the debate about the Affordable Care Act, the public was generally supportive of change. Throughout 2009, respondents in a Kaiser Tracking Poll were asked "Do you think the country as a whole would be better off or worse off if the President and Congress passed health care reform, or don't you think it would make much difference?" Support for reform was strong throughout 2009 and only at the start of 2010 did it fall below a majority.[3] Policies aimed at eliminating restrictions for preexisting conditions and lifetime caps on health benefits had public support and made their way into the Act. However, as the details about the Affordable Care Act began to emerge (sometimes erroneously as the "death panels" example illustrates), public support wavered. The "public option" (providing a government-managed health insurance program as an option for individuals to choose) was controversial and eventually failed to attract majority support by the public. At the time it passed, support for the bill was generally soft, and different ways of framing the bill in survey questions (its impact on the respondent versus on the nation, for example) could lead to majority support or opposition.

Despite the complexity of the issue and the length of the debate in Congress and in media, a Pew poll found that nearly 90 percent of Americans paid at least some attention to the issue (Pew Research Center 2009). Not surprisingly, there were clear differences in partisan support for health care legislation with 59 percent of Democrats supporting legislation and 79 percent of Republicans opposed. The same Pew poll found that there were also partisan differences in attention to the issue with 61 percent of "Conservative Republicans" paying "a lot" of attention compared to 48 percent of "Liberal Democrats."

★ ★ ★

Although the health care bill was landmark legislation and thus not an ordinary political event, it nonetheless serves as a useful starting point for thinking about the larger topic of this book: what collective political judgment looks like in a political context. First, the public did respond to incoming information. Support for health care reform changed once details of the bill began to circulate—that is the public learned and processed information about the health care bill. Some of the provisions were welcomed by the public at large, including the new rules about preexisting conditions, elimination of caps on lifetime costs, and an extension of the age at which dependents remain on their parents' policy. Others, of course, were controversial and did not enjoy wide public support, such as the requirement that adults without employer-based health insurance must buy it, the federal government serving as one of the options that people could choose (what became known as the "public option"), requirements on businesses with more than 50 employees to provide health insurance, and others. But the key point is that public opinion as a whole changed as details about the bill were publicized.

Second, it is important to consider how this information was processed and to note that partisanship played a fundamental role in the information processing. As noted above, Republicans reported being more attentive to the issue than Democrats. This partisan difference in information acquisition is consistent with individual-level studies that describe the public's reliance on motivated reasoning. Motivated reasoning leads people to seek out information that is consistent with their predispositions so that Democrats would not need much evidence to support a bill that was generally framed as "Democratic," whereas Republicans seemed to have been actively seeking out reasons to be suspicious of the bill, something that they use to justify their innate skepticism of Democratic policy initiatives. At times this motivated reasoning leads citizens astray, as is evident by the willingness of some Republicans to believe the death panel rumors circulating during the health care debate. In an August 2009 Pew survey, 47 percent of Republicans believed that the death panels existed as opposed to 28 percent of Independents. At the same time, Democrats were more or less inoculated from these rumors, with only 20 percent reporting that they thought the death panels existed and 64 percent responding that these claims were not true (as compared to 51 percent of Independents and 30 percent of Republicans).[4]

Finally, during the debate about the Affordable Care Act, the public did not seem to be neatly divided into those who were attentive and those who were inattentive, since nearly all respondents in polls reported paying at least some attention to the issues.

But this case shows that even a policy problem as consequential and contentious as health care ebbs and flows in terms of its importance in the mind of the public. According to a Gallup poll taken January 2010, 23 percent of the public rated health care among the "most important problems" facing the nation, but by December 2010, only 8 percent rated it as a most important problem (Gallup Polls January and December 2010). This suggests that there are information channels that have some bearing on the evolution of collective opinion, since the importance that people attach to new information will be influenced by the context in which it is received (i.e., whether the issue is salient or not at the time the information is delivered).

Thus, what emerges from this case are three key factors that must be accounted for in order to understand the dynamics of public opinion—information, partisanship, and salience. Partisanship plays a central role in aggregate opinion, since nearly all political attitudes are filtered through partisan lenses.[5] Since there are only two major parties in the American political system, partisanship reduces the dimensionality of politics, creating a simpler information environment for ordinary citizens. Simplifying the decision-making process is reasonable for citizens, since their lives are occupied by a variety of tasks, many of which take precedence over acquiring and processing information about politics. At the same time, this simplification of the information environment runs the risk of citizens relying so heavily on partisan cues that "real world" information might play a minor role in the formation of collective opinion (Druckman, Peterson & Slothuus 2013). In a related way, the structure of the political system with periodic and partisan elections can interact with partisan predispositions to alter the evolution of collective opinion. For example, it is likely that the dynamics of public opinion will shift on some issues simply by virtue of a transition from one party to the other as a consequence of popular elections. Finally, despite the vast supply of information in modern society, the amount of news that can be absorbed and used by the public is still constrained, forcing issues onto and off of the political agenda.

This conceptualization of aggregate public opinion as structured by partisanship, salience, institutions, and information runs counter to the typical characterization of *collective* opinion. The conventional approach rests on the idea that the public is divided into an attentive and inattentive public, with the attentive public bringing order and meaning to public opinion and the errors of the inattentive public counterbalancing each other and averaging out (Erikson, MacKuen & Stimson 2002). Thus, we are left with aggregate public opinion that is logical and coherent because enough people pay attention to make it that way. Although this idea has strong normative appeal, it is a bit too tidy, washing away many of the key features of political decision-making—most importantly partisanship. The aim of this book is to demonstrate that aggregate public opinion is driven by many of the key features of politics, like partisanship, elections, issue salience, and learning over time. Importantly, what emerges from this messy process is collective political opinion that is still meaningful and coherent despite the public's deviation from strict notions of rationality.[6]

Attentive and Inattentive Publics

The notion of an inattentive public is derived from individual-level studies of public opinion and the failure of many individuals to live up to the standards of meaningful political decision-making. In his early empirical study of public opinion, Walter Lippmann (1922) paints a grim portrait of the electorate, one in which citizens possess little information about the political system and only provide weak signals about the direction that the country should take. And starting with *The American Voter* (Campbell, Converse, Miller & Stokes 1960) and for decades thereafter, political scientists used surveys to document further what Lippmann found—namely, that many Americans lack the knowledge or ideological framework for meaningful political decision-making. Such studies have long been a source of concern for those interested in a healthy, democratic polity, one that responds coherently to salient political issues and holds its leaders accountable.

The idea of an "attentive public" arose from those studying aggregate opinion, and it provided both an alternative conceptualization of collective opinion and a normative defense of it. In *The Rational Public,* Page and Shapiro (1992) argue that public opinion follows reasonable and predictable patterns over time, despite the fact that individual citizens may lack the requisite knowledge to make good decisions. They argue that the public includes many citizens who fit the unflattering image of the electorate described by Lippmann and others, but through the "miracle of aggregation" collective public opinion becomes stable and meaningful as random errors among uninformed citizens cancel out. Extending this line of thought, Erikson, MacKuen, and Stimson (2002) and Stimson (2004, 14–17) contend that within the public enough people are attentive and informed to bring order and stability to aggregate public opinion.[7] Thus, the unstable opinions of those with limited information about politics introduce random noise into the system, while the informed public produces a consistent signal that brings order and meaning to aggregate public opinion. The rationality of the system rests on there being enough people who are knowledgeable about politics to overcome the random errors introduced from those with little or no information about salient political issues.

These contrasting portraits of citizens as both informed and uninformed, rational and irrational, coherent and incoherent are of long-standing interest to political scientists. Those who study politics at the individual level continue to find evidence that citizens do not know key facts that are essential to making sound judgments. One well-publicized and consequential example is that prior to the invasion of Iraq in 2003, 79 percent of the American public believed that Saddam Hussein had supported Al-Qaeda's terrorist activities, when he had not (*Los Angeles Times* 2002). However, those who look at aggregate public opinion over time find evidence to confirm the more optimistic view of the public. For example, in 2008, the public held an historically low view of the economy when it became evident that the problems with the subprime mortgage markets were spreading to the economy at large.

Despite the appeal of the "attentive public" argument, the simple emergence of a rational public from the ill-formed opinions of individual citizens is disputed. Research by Bartels (1996) and Althaus (2003) looks more systematically at this disconnect between macro and micro studies and uses individual-level data to examine the extent to which aggregation overcomes individual-level errors. On the whole, their findings provide little evidence to support the miracle of aggregation. Using simulation techniques, they show that if the public were better informed, collective opinion would be different than what is observed in typical opinion polls—in other words, individual errors do not neatly cancel out. Likewise, the argument that the attentive public provides a coherent link between information in the environment and public opinion is challenged by research showing that citizens typically engage in motivated reasoning. Rather than treating information neutrally, people look for information that confirms their existing views and discount information that is contrary to their opinions (Taber & Lodge 2006). But, it turns out that those who are most sophisticated (i.e., those whom we depend upon most to bring rationality to the system) are actually best at using motivated reasoning and most partisan. Therefore, the attentive public is more likely to view politics through a partisan lens and able to use new information to confirm their existing views and discount information that runs contrary to them (Gaines et al. 2007).

These critics contend that to understand collective public opinion requires a new conceptualization of aggregate opinion, one that moves beyond the idea of an attentive and inattentive public to one that is better grounded in the exigencies of modern mass democracy. Thus, the challenge is to understand how aggregate political opinion is updated when the public is comprised of partisans with shifting attention to issues, unanticipated events alter the political landscape (referred to here as regime changes), and elections reconfigure political responsibilities.

Modeling Aggregate Opinion

The conventional understanding of macro political behavior is derived from a stimulus–response model. A stimulus–response model is grounded on the idea that changes in public opinion respond straightforwardly to changes in the political and economic environment.[8] For example, the impact of a change in unemployment is the same whether it occurs in 1985, under a Republican president, or in 1995, under a Democratic president. In addition, most studies of aggregate opinion ignore or assume away the role of partisanship as a factor in the dynamics of aggregate opinion.[9] The aim of this book is to develop a model of information processing that is consistent with the exigencies of mass democracy, namely, that the public's attention is diverted by other things, which leads to decision-making that relies on common heuristics, shifting attention, information flows, and partisanship. This means that the public as a whole falls short of the ideal "rational" decision-maker but nonetheless learns from changes in the environment, makes judgments in accordance with values, and does not stray too far from the views of experts when making evaluations of economic conditions (as demonstrated in a benchmarking analysis described in Chapter 6.)

Moving from a stimulus–response model to an information-processing model requires a description of the updating process—that is, how the public as a whole takes in information and uses it to update public sentiment in light of news. Social scientists have increasingly relied on models of Bayesian updating to explain the process by which information is used in the formation of attitudes and opinions, and Bayesian updating corresponds with much of our understanding and intuition about how information gets used by the public. The basic idea behind any updating model is to describe decision-making over time as new information becomes available.[10] The distinguishing feature of a Bayesian updating model is the assumption that decision-makers approach an issue with some prior understanding and that this understanding carries some weight when the public updates its opinion. For example, if people are asked about the likelihood that a new flu strain will create a pandemic, their responses are likely to be influenced by their perceptions of recent flu scares like H1N1. But an additional assumption for Bayesian updating is that the uncertainty about the prior matters as well. In general, people's assessments of flu outbreaks (i.e., their priors) will be more uncertain than their assessments about changes in gas prices, since the latter is something they routinely encounter and make judgments about. On issues in which the public has more uncertainty, new information carries more weight; whereas when decision-making is about issues in which the public has more certainty (i.e., stronger priors), new information is less likely to dramatically alter existing perceptions.

The role of priors gets more complicated (but is a more realistic starting point) when partisanship is introduced. For example, on an issue like the "surge" strategy that President Obama proposed for Afghanistan in December 2009, the public's views about the likely effectiveness of this strategy will be influenced by people's prior perceptions about the effectiveness of the "surge" strategy employed by President Bush in Iraq and people's partisanship. Republicans were likely to be favorably disposed to the "surge strategy" since it first arose as a strategy under the George W. Bush administration. But, in 2009, would Democrats endorse the surge because President Obama proposed it or be suspicious about it because of its association with the Bush administration? The results of a Cable News Network (CNN) poll in December 2009 show about equal level of support among partisans for a "surge" strategy in Afghanistan (CNN/Opinion Research Corporation 2009). It is difficult to know for certain that Republican support for the policy was a byproduct of their association of the strategy with the one that President Bush employed in Iraq, but the majority support among Republicans is at least consistent with that interpretation. Likewise, Democrats had generally been opposed to an expanded role for the military in Iraq and Afghanistan, but seemed to rally behind President Obama with regard to this initiative.

The fundamental features of the Bayesian model comport nicely with the logic of the "rational public" as described by Page and Shapiro (1992), Erikson, MacKuen, and Stimson (2002), and Stimson (2004) but adds to it the idea that the public weighs news or novel information. Page and Shapiro (1992, 15–16) argue that "new information, some enduring but some transient and quickly contradicted, may push an individual's preferences back and forth in a seemingly random fashion," but there is a core attitude around which these fluctuations occur. However, the Bayesian updating model suggests that information may not "push" expressed opinion around in the way that Page and Shapiro describe. Instead, the response to new information will be guided by the prior level of certainty or uncertainty regarding the issue at hand. For example, if the economy has grown steadily and the public has consistently responded in public opinion polls that the incumbent president is doing a good job managing the economy, a report of lower home sales is weighed against the steady stream of good news that preceded it. Since the overall trend in the news was positive, there is no reason for the public to re-evaluate markedly its assessment of the president's management of the economy. However, if economic conditions were in flux, the public is likely to respond quickly to new information about a downturn in the economy and respond equally quickly to news about an economic recovery. The summer of 2008, just before the severity of the financial crisis became apparent, provides a good example of the economy in flux. Financial markets were in turmoil and unemployment was rising but the stock market was not yet in a steep decline (in contrast to the fall, when reports of dramatic drops in stock prices occurred almost daily). Under such conditions, there is likely to be a good deal of volatility in the public's evaluation of the economy because of the underlying uncertainty.

Some studies of individual-level opinion argue that the demands of Bayesian updating are too high for ordinary citizens to meet (Kim, Taber & Lodge 2010). The contention is that partisanship, in particular, leads ordinary citizens to place too much weight on their prior opinions, making them less likely to update in light of new information. However, in the analysis of aggregate opinion over time (as in this book), persistence of opinion has long been a focus of study and can be easily integrated into an updating model. In addition, as Bullock (2009) suggests, whether or not ordinary citizens fully meet the standards of Bayesian updating, it is a useful way to study information processing since it provides a means to examine the weight that new information plays in the formulation of public opinion over time. Finally, it is possible to modify the Bayesian updating framework to account for systematic deviations from pure Bayesian updating. The models of Bayesian updating are very flexible and this flexibility facilitates the incorporation of many of the unique features of collective political decision-making into the analysis, such as institutional changes, regime shifts, partisanship, and changes in information flow. In addition, the flexibility of these models means that these political factors may play important roles in some settings but not in others. For example, in Chapter 4, the methods of estimating a Bayesian updating model will be specified in a way that facilitates the estimation of "persistence" in public opinion arising from partisanship.

Components of Collective Political Rationality

In each of the chapters in this book, I examine the key factors thought to influence collective public opinion and show how they can be incorporated into a Bayesian updating model. The key factors examined here are random and non-random errors, partisanship, information (or news), and events. Once these components are examined individually, I show the role that they play in collective opinion when taken together. Through this process, I demonstrate the important role that political factors, particularly partisanship, play in aggregate opinion over time.

Random and Non-Random Error (or a Critique of Aggregation)

Although individual-level studies of voting and public opinion document the ways in which individual citizens make errors in political judgments through inattention, misinformation, or miscalculation (Campbell et al. 1960), aggregate studies describe the implications of these errors for the public as a whole. A central argument for those defending collective rationality is that public opinion contains a clear signal (informed judgments) and that the errors (uninformed judgments) evident in micro-level studies will cancel out (i.e., errors are as likely to be positive as negative and their net effect is zero). As noted above, the source of that signal is generally thought to be those who are attentive to politics. However, given that the "attentive" public is also the "partisan" public, there are reasons to be skeptical of this simple formulation of signal and noise. These issues are examined in Chapter 2. There I more fully assess the nature of the signal, the size of the error, and the importance of the signal-to-noise ratio for understanding collective public opinion over time. The size of the signal relative to the errors is important to consider since even if the errors cancel, they may be so large that they drown out any detectable signal and we are still left with collective opinion that is effectively noise.[11]

Party

Although partisanship is a well-documented source of bias and distortion, it is also the edifice upon which most political opinions and decisions rest (Bartels 2002, Kull, Ramsay & Lewis 2003, Bartels 2009). For scholars of elections, this is an uncontroversial claim. Partisanship continues to be a dominant factor in nearly every voting decision (Lewis-Beck et al. 2008), and is perhaps the only basis for judgment in low-information elections like state representative. For those looking at public opinion across time and between elections, this is a more provocative claim. Those who have argued for collective rationality contend that partisanship plays a minimal role in the aggregate because partisans update their opinions in parallel (Erikson, MacKuen & Stimson 2002). That is, when Democrats view the president less favorably because of poor job performance, Republicans will as well, no matter what the party of the incumbent president is. Partisans will have different mean levels of support depending on the party of the incumbent, but their support will shift in tandem, yielding distinct but parallel judgments about the president.

Despite the reassurances of Page and Shapiro and others (Erikson, MacKuen & Stimson 2002), this remains a controversial claim. As Bartels (2002) shows in his panel study of partisan bias, in issue after issue, from assessments about unemployment to social security, the movement of partisans is not parallel. In light of this counter-evidence, it is clear that partisanship does not disappear as part of the miracle of aggregation, and this requires saying why partisanship matters for aggregate opinion. Partisanship is a familiar lens through which the public views political issues and one of the ostensible virtues of partisanship is that it conveys to citizens information about candidates or issues to help them make decisions. Given its role in elections, the importance of partisanship should be as profound when citizens are asked about political issues between elections and their attention is more likely to be diverted away from politics. On economic matters, partisanship arises when Democrats are less likely to signal their disapproval with a Democratic president in response to bad economic news. Likewise, Republicans might be reluctant to say that they approve of the job that Democratic presidents are doing, despite positive news about presidential performance (McAvoy & Enns 2010, Evans & Pickup 2010). Or the influence of partisanship might mean that it takes more good or bad news to move partisans. For example, Taber and Lodge (2006) use experimental data to show that people tend to scrutinize information that is at odds with their current beliefs and accept without much consideration information that confirms their existing predispositions, particularly when elite political cues are available (Druckman, Peterson & Slothuus 2013).

In Chapter 3, I disaggregate key time series about aggregate public opinion, like presidential approval and assessments of economic conditions, in order to show the way that partisanship influences the dynamics of collective opinion, focusing on the dynamics of the in-party (the party aligned with the president) and the out-party (the party opposing the president). I show how they evolve in ways consistent with micro-level theories like motivated reasoning rather than in ways consistent with the miracle of aggregation. However, I argue that the influence of partisanship does not diminish the quality of aggregate opinion.[12]

Information

For a variety of reasons, aggregate models of behavior are generally grounded on assumptions of perfect or near-perfect information processing. Often these assumptions are justified as necessary simplifications, but at times, they reflect researchers' convictions that at least some individuals are able to perform the demanding task of "rationally" processing the vast amounts of information in the current media-rich environment. However, individual-level studies suggest that rather than acting as systematic information processors, citizens try to interpret facts to fit their existing view points, and those who are more informed tend to be better at incorporating new information into their existing interpretation of political affairs (Gaines et al. 2007, Duch, Palmer & Anderson 2000). With new and complex issues making their way to the top of the political agenda, it is not surprising that citizens, even well-intentioned ones, rely on party cues and other information shortcuts to sift through the wealth of information in the modern political environment. Thus, even those engaged with politics may not comport with idealized notions of rational citizens, and as a result may ignore some information while being attentive (or at times overly attentive) to other sources of information.

In addition, when looking over time at issues that capture the public's attention, the prominence of any particular issue is going to ebb and flow. Despite the fact that there is a constant stream of economic information published by government agencies, media reporting about the economy varies, in part from economic cycles and trends, but also because of the salience of other issues that compete for prominence on the agenda. A shift in salience will influence the issues that will be weighed most heavily in updating evaluations of the economy, assessment of presidents, or the performance of other political institutions, such as Congress or the Supreme Court. These issues of selective attention and an analysis of the time-varying impact of issues are examined in Chapter 4.

Regime Changes

We know that partisan bias does not occur consistently across time. As many studies have shown, during times of crisis Americans of both parties tend to "rally around the flag" and signal their support for the president in unison. In addition, Lavine, Johnston, and Steenbergen (2012) argue that partisan loyalty does periodically erode when the other party is doing things right for an extended period of time. For example, during the economic boom of the late 1990s, Republicans generally acknowledged that economic conditions were improving and that Clinton was doing a good job managing the economy. Lavine, Johnston, and Steenbergen (2012) show that those without strong party loyalties—the people that they call "ambivalent partisans"—are most likely to change their point of view with a steady stream of good news.

There are a variety of factors built into the political system that can dramatically alter the trajectory of public opinion. For example, events like elections can redirect opinion along a new path, and for some public opinion series, like presidential approval, this type of change is well documented through studies of presidential transitions and honeymoon periods. In addition, changes to public opinion can arise from unexpected events (as opposed to anticipated events like elections and "honeymoons") and these can play a role in updating as well. Some of these events have an enduring impact on opinion, like the Iraq War, and others can have dramatic, yet transitory effects, like President Reagan's decision to invade Grenada.

Changes to opinion that are not predictable from outside events can also occur. Expectations about the future, particularly about the economy, can take on a life of their own, building momentum and taking opinion to unexpected highs and lows. This type of change is notably absent from most studies of aggregate opinion, yet it can have profound consequences on the direction of opinions on a variety of topics. In Chapter 3, I examine the impact of these events in the context of partisanship and explore their impact more broadly when analyzing regime-change models in Chapter 5.

Research Design

Level of Analysis

If we knew that the number of people capable of making reasoned decisions about politics was near zero, we would know that democratic governance was nearly impossible and look for some other way to organize nation-states. If we knew that all citizens were fully informed about politics, we could feel very confident about the prospects for democratic governance and know to take public opinion seriously. Any public is surely somewhere in between these two extremes, and given this messy middle ground, we are forced to think seriously about the legitimacy of public opinion and the utility of democratic governance. Framing the study of public opinion this way leads naturally to the study of aggregate public opinion over time, rather than individual-level analysis. Given the polarization of the current time period, it is readily apparent that the impact of partisanship will not be the same over time. What this means in terms of analysis, however, is that we need to study partisanship and its influence on aggregate opinion over time; another individual-level survey is not really going to help us understand the role of partisanship on opinion. This fluctuation in the influence of partisanship is in part due to elites providing partisan cues. If party leaders generally disagree, this elite polarization will increase the strength of partisan signals to the public and the role of partisanship in aggregate opinion should increase (Layman, Carsey & Horowitz 2006, Druckman, Peterson & Slothuus 2012, Bolsen, Druckman & Cook 2014, Levendusky 2009). In other words, to understand these foundational issues about the coherence of public opinion, we don't really want to try to determine what percent of the population is knowledgeable about politics at a particular moment in time. Instead we want to know whether public opinion, when taken as a whole, is orderly and meaningful over time, particularly since it is aggregate level opinion to which political leaders pay attention (Druckman & Leeper 2012). This has led those studying aggregate opinion to focus most of their attention on the movement in public opinion over time and to determine its coherence.

Despite the importance of aggregate opinion to the study of democratic politics, it is a mistake to ignore or minimize the influence of micro-level factors, like partisanship and political knowledge. These factors should play a role in the movement (or dynamics) of public opinion as well. Thus, to fully understand the movement in opinion, it is necessary to examine events and changes in political and economic conditions but to also incorporate influences like partisanship and political knowledge into the analysis as well. An alternative way to approach this issue of why micro-level factors remain important in aggregate studies is to think about the types of errors that the public makes when reasoning about politics. The conventional argument for those studying public opinion as a whole is that individual citizens make random errors that cancel out in the aggregate. If partisanship is operative, things work a little differently. Partisanship provides people information and thus reduces errors. But sometimes the errors that remain are systematic rather than random. As noted before, there were very few Democrats—even low-information ones—who believed that the legislation for the ACA included provisions for "death panels." Yet a sizable number of Republicans believed that they would exist. In this case, partisanship led both low- and high-information Democrats to be suspicious of these rumors, leaving only some Republicans to believe them. Thus, we are reducing random error but introducing some systematic error. If the systematic error is small, and the potential random error is large, this is a good tradeoff. If the systematic error is large, we've just traded off one kind of error for another with no real net benefit and perhaps a net loss.

Polls

It is clear that public opinion plays a central role in establishing how well-suited American citizens are to democratic governance, but its status as a barometer of an effective democratic system deserves some scrutiny. Prior to the evolution of the public opinion poll, voting was the key activity by which citizen performance could be judged. Citizens were expected to make informed judgments and be apprised of current issues at the time of regularly scheduled elections and their typical two-year cycle. Tuning in to current events and political debates every two years seems luxurious when compared to today's nonstop politics, with near continuous presidential election campaigns, twenty-four hour news cycles, and ongoing fundraising by members of Congress.

Although voting continues to be a key benchmark for citizen performance both in the political system and in political science research, the rise of public opinion polls means it is feasible to assess citizen competence more often and, thus, this makes the job of being an informed citizen a decidedly more demanding one. George Gallup, a pioneer in the field of polling, hoped that the public opinion poll would aid the democratic process by providing citizens an opportunity to contribute to governing the country in an ongoing way, rather than just periodically as in elections.

> In my opinion, modern polls are the chief hope of lifting government to a higher level ... Polls can make government more efficient and responsive ... they can make us a truer democracy.[13]

The difficulty for citizens, however, is that in order to look competent, they are now expected to have coherent opinions on issues as wide-ranging as military strikes in Syria to the threat of domestic terrorism to the performance of the Supreme Court.

Relatedly, the issues and the frequency with which the public is polled influences assessments about the quality of public opinion. There are polls that regularly ask citizens about familiar issues, like economic conditions and presidential performance, but then there are topics that are unfamiliar, such as the threat that mad cow disease in Britain poses to American consumers of beef. On familiar issues, measured opinions are often partisan and, as Druckman, Peterson, and Slothuus (2012) note, polls on these issues tend to show that public opinion exhibits stability over time. However, in this age in which public opinion polls figure prominently in political discussions and decisions, pollsters also want to capture public opinion at particular moments in time, so when unique events arrive on the political agenda, like the Ebola threat of 2014, citizens get asked about these issues. But since many of these are unfamiliar issues, there can be a high degree of instability in public opinion. Each new piece of information can lead to dramatic shifts in public attitudes. The updating model described here makes it easier to account for these differences in the prior information that people bring to political issues and to better account for instability that is inherent in asking the public about topics about which people are not very familiar.

Data

In order to study collective political rationality, I rely on some unique as well as some familiar data sources. The presidential approval series, first introduced as a survey question in the 1930s by the Gallup organization, is surely *the* most studied public opinion question. Despite its familiarity and the extensive analysis of it, the series continues to serve as a valuable mechanism for studying aggregate public opinion. Because evaluation of the president is an inherently partisan assessment, the series captures many of the key institutional, social, economic, and foreign policy changes that influence aggregate public opinion.[14] If we think of picking cases to study the impact of politics on aggregate opinion, this could be categorized as an easy case. Nonetheless, easy cases—studied systematically—can be informative and generative.

A harder case for assessing the nature of collective *political* judgments is an evaluation of the economy. Since economic considerations dominate much of discourse and evaluation of politics, the economy is a topic to which most citizens pay attention and get updated information. In addition, the question of economic evaluations does not raise obvious partisan cues in the way that questions about the performance of Congress might (e.g., Democrats would be more likely to have a favorable view of Congress if their party controlled the House and Senate). In other words, given that there is a "real economy" to evaluate, it is a harder test of partisan effects than a series with more obvious partisan cues. In order to assess the impact of partisanship in this case, I compiled a unique dataset. Going back to the original polls from Gallup, CBS, and ABC, I disaggregated economic evaluations by party from 1989 to 2012 and these are an important part of the analysis in Chapters 3 and 4. In addition, I disaggregated economic evaluations by party and education and these are shown in Chapter 2. Although looking at data disaggregated by party has become more common (Lebo & Cassino 2007, McAvoy & Enns 2010), the ultimate goal is to understand the role that partisanship plays in collective public opinion and, in particular, its impact on collective political rationality.

Political Rationality

Given the divisiveness and intransigence of contemporary American politics, the idea of collective political rationality might seem an unattainable goal. However, investigations into the nature of collective and individual political rationality constitute one of the enduring questions in the study of politics and remain central today even in an era of intense partisanship (Levendusky 2009), elite divisiveness (Binder 2003), and segmented information (Prior 2007).

Within political science, rationality is widely discussed, but what is meant by the term remains elusive—with scholars in different fields emphasizing different aspects of it or providing different definitions. Early studies of public opinion and its rationality, such as those by Lippmann (1922), sought evidence that the public was informed on important matters of the day (and were sorely disappointed by what they found). In this view, collective rationality arises from an informed public. Building on this idea of citizen rationality but using a more systematic study of public opinion, Campbell et al. (1960) confirmed that many citizens lacked basic knowledge of political institutions and issues of the day, and these problems were compounded by the absence of a reliable ideological framework to make sense of specific issues and provide consistency across issues. Thus, for these scholars, rationality is evident when large swaths of the public act like ideal, democratic citizens—informed, attentive, and ideologically consistent.

Political psychologists approach the issue of citizen rationality and competence in a different way, abandoning the standard expectations about how citizens *should* make decisions and focusing their attention on how citizens do make decisions. Thus, they changed the standards of judgment from "what an ideal citizen might decide" to one in which the we seek to find those aspects of human decision-making that facilitate choice and allow people to attain their goals, either for themselves or the public at large (Lupia, McCubbins & Popkin 2000). This line of inquiry has been productive and allowed scholars to ground their understanding of political decision-making in the milieu of modern society. Thus, individual citizens are not expected to be rational calculators who search extensively for information to make proper judgments about an ongoing list of issues at the top of the political agenda. Instead, the approach is to take citizens as they are and to recognize that individual citizens (even the most motivated and informed) only devote part of their attention to political decision-making and as a result make decisions using strategies that help them cut through the plethora of information available to them. Numerous studies have demonstrated that heuristics, cue-taking, habits, and motivated reasoning can lead to decision making that allows citizens to make choices that are consistent with their goals (Lau & Redlawsk 2006). From this view of rationality, ordinary citizens can meet the demands of large-scale democratic politics.

Another defense of political rationality (alluded to in the discussion of the attentive and inattentive public) emphasizes the role of aggregation in overcoming individual-level errors. The standard of rationality employed in this defense is to search for consistency between changes in the environment and changes in aggregate opinion. As Page and Shapiro (1992, 53) argue,

> the changes [in public opinion] do not move in helter-skelter fashion but instead respond sensibly to changes in information and changes in reality.

Thus, by comparing collective opinion to known changes in the environment, we learn that individual errors do not add up to a collective opinion that is chaotic and unpredictable. Although there are reasons to take this approach seriously, it also has notable shortcomings. The principal one is that unlike the defense offered above, there is little in the way of political decision-making at work.[15] The miracle of aggregation is as applicable to decisions about buying computers as it is to choosing candidates, but in the end, it washes away much of what we understand as the foundations of *political* decision-making, partisanship, information shortcuts, learning, and so on.

The Bayesian updating model utilized in the analysis in this book is related more to models of bounded rationality than strict rationality; this seems to more clearly reflect the realities of political decision-making. Neither citizens, nor the public as a whole, thoroughly scrutinize information that comes their way or exhaustively weigh that information as they formulate opinions and make decisions. Instead, new information is influenced by past decisions, partisans will weigh information differently, and the link from information to opinions will change over time. In his defense of models of bounded rationality, Sargent (1993) argues that this view of the decision-making process puts the public and the researchers on the same footing; both are continually trying to determine the "correct" model while adjusting to new information. Therefore, the "true" model may continually shift over time as citizens' preferences shift or as they develop new decision rules. But the process is, nonetheless, consistent with notions of rationality in terms of learning from the environment and making choices consistent with goals.

In the contemporary era, the biggest challenge to the idea of bounded rationality is partisanship. Partisanship would not be necessary or relevant in a world of ideal citizens who studied political news and made unbiased judgments with that information, but few think that this describes contemporary political reality. Given the overwhelming evidence that these purely rational decision-makers are in short supply, what role does party play? As noted above, experimental studies of political decision-making show that rather than studying issues exhaustively, citizens tend to use information shortcuts to facilitate decision-making. Most people are biased information processors, more willing to accept information that confirms their existing view, and this effect is stronger among the politically informed (Taber & Lodge 2006).

If partisanship makes a difference in aggregate public opinion, does this undermine arguments about collective rationality? Not necessarily. If partisanship structures political thinking, then we need to consider what it is contributing and what is being lost as partisan opinion is aggregated. The argument in this book is that partisanship does what it has always done: give citizens—who are not fulltime policy analysts and who fall short of the ideal democratic citizen—a reasonable means to make political decisions. Thus, collective opinion will be biased but far more consistent and potentially more informed, than it would be in the absence of partisan cues. Without partisanship, citizens (both informed and uninformed) would be lost. In other words, we must accept some amount of partisan bias in order to have a better informed electorate. The bias is real but relatively small, allowing the public as a whole (warts and all) to send a consistent signal about its preferences.

Thus, collective political rationality and Bayesian updating implies a much more complex relationship between information, news, and opinion than models of strict rationality suggest. The public does in fact ignore information that comes its way based on prior decisions and the weight of new information. I have argued, however, that this does not undercut the public's claims to be politically rational. Still, it is useful to know how far these deviations from strict rationality push the public away from an evaluation that would occur based on the calculations of a more perfectly "rational" individual. In Chapter 6, I compare the updating behavior of experts (professional economic forecasters) to that of the public. This comparison makes it possible to benchmark the information processing capacity of the public against "rational decision-making." The benchmarking analysis shows that it may be possible to put arguments for collective rationality on a firmer footing.

Summary

Amidst the polarization of contemporary politics, partisan loyalties among citizens are regarded as one contributor to political stalemate. Partisan loyalties lead Democrats and Republicans to look at the same economic information but to come to strikingly different conclusions about the state of the economy and the performance of the president in managing it. As a result, many observers argue that democratic politics would work better if citizens would shed their party loyalty and more dispassionately assess political and economic news. In this book, I argue—contra this conventional wisdom—that partisanship is a necessary feature of modern politics, making it feasible for citizens to make some sense of the vast number of issues that make their way onto the political agenda. Using some unique data, I show that the biases and distortions that partisanship introduces to collective opinion are real, but despite them, collective opinion changes meaningfully in response to economic and political news. In a comparison of the public's assessment of the economy to those of economic experts, I find a close correspondence between the two over time, and this lends support to the main argument in the book: that in modern democracies, an informed public will also necessarily be partisan.

Notes

1. The deal negotiated with Senator Nelson did not make it into the final legislation.
2. Stupak was an anti-abortion Democrat representing an electorally competitive district in Michigan. He chose not to run for reelection in 2010.
3. Kaiser Family Foundation, Kaiser Health Tracking Poll, www.pollingreport.com/health7.htm, accessed October 31, 2014.
4. Pew Research Center Poll, August 14–17, 2009, http://www.pollingreport.com/health6.htm, accessed June 13, 2014.
5. Surveys show that true Independents are exceedingly rare. Most people who identify themselves as Independents lean toward one party in their voting behavior and policy preferences (Keith et al. 1992).
6. Different types of rationality, e.g., strict and bounded, are taken up later in this chapter.
7. Soroka and Wlezien (2010) extend this argument of the legitimacy of aggregate opinion by showing that public officials respond to public opinion, rather than the other way around.
8. Jacobs and Shapiro (2000) add the role of politicians as a factor in the formation of public opinion, arguing that politicians strategically choose issues that are advantageous to them and try to shape public opinion for their benefit.

9. Stimson (2004) does examine subgroups and their role in aggregate opinion, but he stresses the role of those in the middle in moving public opinion. Studies of aggregate opinion by Lebo and Cassino (2007), McAvoy and Enns (2010), Enns and McAvoy (2012), and Enns, Kellstedt, and McAvoy (2012) show the role that partisanship plays in the movement of aggregate opinion.
10. This means describing how change occurs as we move from one point in time to another. A least-squares approach to updating implies that the public takes new information as a new data point in a regression model and re-estimates the weight of new information as part of the full history of a decision. Thus, in a model of presidential approval, changes to unemployment that occurred in the 1960s share the same weight in an estimate of current approval as more recent data.
11. Page and Shapiro (1992) recognize that a detectable "signal" is necessary for their "rational public" argument, but they don't systematically assess the strength of the signal relative to the errors, primarily because they don't estimate the size of the errors.
12. For a normative defense of partisanship, see Rosenblum (2008) and Muirhead (2014).
13. The quote of Gallup is from Asher (2011, 49).
14. It should be noted that there have been numerous attempts to make the case that the dynamics of presidential approval are not partisan, see for example Erikson, MacKuen, and Stimson (2002, 71–73). However, the sharp partisan differences that emerged during the George W. Bush administration and continued into the Obama administration have effectively ended this debate (Jacobson 2006).
15. Page and Shapiro (1992, 17) do note that the connection between policy opinion and changes in the environment is likely the byproduct of things like heuristics and cue-taking from political leaders, but they do not examine the ways in which this type of decision-making plays out in collective opinion change.

Bibliography

Althaus, Scott L. 2003. *Collective Preferences in Democratic Politics*. Cambridge: Cambridge University Press.

Asher, Herbert B. 2011. *Polling and the Public: What Every Citizens Should Know*. Washington DC: CQ Press.

Bartels, Larry. 1996. "Uninformed Voters: Information Effects in Presidential Elections." *American Journal of Political Science* 40(1):194–230.

Bartels, Larry. 2002. "Beyond the Running Tally: Partisan Bias in Political Perceptions." *Political Behavior* 24(2):117–150.

Bartels, Larry M. 2009. *Unequal Democracy: The Political Economy of the New Gilded Age*. Princeton, NJ: Princeton University Press.

Binder, Sarah A. 2003. *Stalemate: Causes and Consequences of Legislative Gridlock*. Washington, DC: Brookings Institution Press.

Bolsen, Toby, James N. Druckman & Fay Lomax Cook. 2014. "The Influence of Partisan Motivated Reasoning on Public Opinion." *Political Behavior* 36(2):235–262.

Bullock, John G. 2009. "Partisan Bias and the Bayesian Ideal in the Study of Public Opinion." *Journal of Politics* 71(3):1109–24.

Campbell, Angus, Philip E. Converse, Warren E. Miller & Donald E. Stokes. 1960. *The American Voter*. New York: Wiley.

CNN/Opinion Research Corporation. 2009. "The Roper Center for Public Opinion Research, University of Connecticut." December. Retrieved November 1, 2014 from the iPOLL Databank.

Druckman, James N. & Thomas J. Leeper. 2012. "Is Public Opinion Stable? Resolving the Micro/Macro Disconnect in Studies of Public Opinion." *Daedalus* 141(4):50–68.

Druckman, James N., Erik Peterson & Rune Slothuus. 2012. "A Source of Bias in Public Opinion Stability." *The American Political Science Review* 106(2):430–454.

Druckman, James N., Erik Peterson & Rune Slothuus. 2013. "How Elite Partisan Polarization Affects Public Opinion Formation." *The American Political Science Review* 107(1):57–79.

Duch, Raymond M., Harvey D. Palmer & Christopher Anderson. 2000. "Heterogeneity in Perceptions of National Economic Conditions." *American Journal of Political Science* 44(4):635–652.

Enns, Peter K. & Gregory E. McAvoy. 2012. "The Role of Partisanship in Aggregate Opinion." *Political Behavior* 34(4):627–651.

Enns, Peter K., Paul M. Kellstedt & Gregory E. McAvoy. 2012. "The Consequences of Partisanship in Economic Perceptions." *Public Opinion Quarterly* 76(2):287–310.

Erikson, Robert S., Michael B. MacKuen & James A. Stimson. 2002. *The Macro Polity.* New York: Cambridge University Press.

Evans, Geoffrey & Mark Pickup. 2010. "Reversing the Causal Arrow: The Political Conditioning of Economic Perceptions in the 2000–2004 U.S. Presidential Election Cycle." *The Journal of Politics* 72(4):1236–1251.

Gaines, Brian J., James H. Kuklinski, Paul J. Quirk, Buddy Peyton & Jay Verkuilen. 2007. "Same Facts, Different Interpretations: Partisan Motivation and Opinion on Iraq." *Journal of Politics* 69(4):957–974.

Gallup Polls. 2010. "The Roper Center for Public Opinion Research, University of Connecticut." January and December. Retrieved June 3, 2011 from the iPOLL Databank.

Jacobs, Lawrence R. & Robert Y. Shapiro. 2000. *Politicians Don't Pander: Political Manipulation and the Loss of Democratic Responsiveness.* Chicago, IL: University of Chicago Press.

Jacobs, Lawrence R. & Theda Skocpol. 2010. *Health Care Reform and American Politics: What Everyone Needs to Know.* New York: Oxford University Press.

Jacobson, Gary C. 2006. *Divider, Not a Uniter: George W. Bush and the American People.* New York: Pearson Longman.

Keith, Bruce E., David B. Magleby, Candice J. Nelson, Elizabeth Orr & Mark C.C. Westlye. 1992. *The Myth of the Independent Voter.* Berkeley, CA: University of California Press.

Kim, Sung-youn, Charles S. Taber & Milton Lodge. 2010. "A Computational Model of the Citizen as Motivated Reasoner: Modeling the Dynamics of the 2000 Presidential Election." *Political B* 32(1):1–28.

Kull, Steven, Clay Ramsay & Evan Lewis. 2003. "Misperceptions, the Media, and the Iraq war." *Political Science Quarterly* 118(4):569–598.

Lau, Richard R. & David P. Redlawsk. 2006. *How Voters Decide: Information Processing during Election Campaigns.* Cambridge: Cambridge University Press.

Lavine, Howard G., Christopher D. Johnston & Marco R. Steenbergen. 2012. *The Ambivalent Partisan: How Critical Loyalty Promotes Democracy.* Oxford: Oxford University Press.

Layman, Geoffrey C, Thomas M Carsey & Juliana Menasce Horowitz. 2006. "Party polarization in American politics: Characteristics, Causes, and Consequences." *Annual Review of Political Science* 9:83–110.

Lebo, Matthew. J. & Daniel. Cassino. 2007. "The Aggregated Consequences of Motivated Reasoning and the Dynamics of Partisan Presidential Approval." *Political Psychology* 28(6):719–746.

Levendusky, Matthew. 2009. *The Partisan Sort*. Chicago, IL: University of Chicago Press.

Lewis-Beck, Michael S., William G. Jacoby, Helmut Norpoth & Herbert F. Weisberg. 2008. *The American Voter Revisited*. Ann Arbor, MI: University of Michigan Press.

Lippmann, Walter. 1922. *Public Opinion*. New York: Macmillan.

Los Angeles Times. 2002. "The Roper Center for Public Opinion Research, University of Connecticut." August Retrieved November 1, 2014 from the iPOLL Databank.

Lupia, Athur, Mathew D. McCubbins & Samuel L. Popkin. 2000. "Beyond Rationality: Reason and the Study of Politics". In *Elements Of Reason: Cognition, Choice, and the Bounds Of Rationality*. Cambridge: Cambridge University Press.

McAvoy, Gregory E. & Peter K. Enns. 2010. "Using Approval of the President's Handling of the Economy to Understand Who Polarizes and Why." *Presidential Studies Quarterly* 40(3):545–558.

Muirhead, Russell. 2014. *The Promise of Party in a Polarized Age*. Cambridge, MA: Harvard University Press.

Page, Benjamin I. & Robert Y. Shapiro. 1992. *The Rational Public: Fifty Years of Trends in Americans' Policy Preferences*. Chicago, IL: University of Chicago Press.

Pew Research Center. 2009. "The Roper Center for Public Opinion Research, University of Connecticut." Retrieved November 1, 2014 from the iPOLL Databank.

Prior, Markus. 2007. *Post-Broadcast Democracy*. Cambridge: Cambridge University Press.

Rosenblum, Nancy L. 2008. *On the Side of the Angels: An Appreciation of Parties and Partisanship*. Princeton, NJ: Princeton University Press.

Sargent, Thomas J. 1993. *Bounded Rationality in Macroeconomics*. New York: Oxford University Press.

Soroka, Stuart N. & Christopher Wlezien. 2010. *Degrees of Democracy: Politics, Public Opinion, and Policy*. Cambridge University Press.

Stimson, James A. 2004. *Tides of Consent: How Public Opinion Shapes American Politics*. New York: Cambridge University Press.

Taber, Charles S. & Milton Lodge. 2006. "Motivated Skepticism in the Evaluation of Political Beliefs." *American Journal of Political Science* 50(3):755–769.

2

PUBLIC OPINION

Signal or Noise?

Even for those immersed in the study of public opinion, it is sometimes difficult to accept the idea that the coherence and meaning of mass democracy rests, at least in some measure, on the aggregation of individual opinion that may be ill-informed. Among the well-documented shortcomings of individual citizens are a lack of basic knowledge of political institutions, the names of elected representatives, the issue positions of candidates, historical facts (e.g., which side the US supported in the Vietnam war) as well as substantial segments of the public clinging to faulty information (e.g., Al-Qaeda was operating in Iraq prior to the US-led invasion, Barack Obama is a Muslim). In addition, surveys reveal that when Americans are asked about key issues, respondents provide what are described as non-attitudes—that is, many respondents provide answers to survey questions but without any clear understanding of the issues (for example, surveys asking people whether US foreign-aid spending should increase or decrease show that most people have no idea how much we actually spend, making it meaningless to ask a question about whether it should increase or decrease.)[1] But, as recounted in James Surowiecki's *The Wisdom of Crowds,* the aggregation of individuals (even though many of them will make errors) lead to coherent prices in the case of markets or public opinion in the case of measured attitudes.

The study of aggregate public opinion builds upon this idea that collective rationality "exists" in the sense that the aggregation of individual opinions constitutes a meaningful representation of collective thought, will, or attitudes. This view parallels the justification for democratic governance and citizen enfranchisement. In voting, there is an implicit belief that despite individual shortcomings, collective will is identifiable, legitimate, and authoritative (with some exceptions, such as when state courts declare citizen initiatives unconstitutional). So, the argument goes, if the collective expression of opinion in voting is legitimate, so too is the collective expression of opinion as collected through public opinion polls.

Of course, the outcome of elections and public opinion polls can be baffling (see foreign aid spending above), and when paired with decades of research on the ways in which citizens fail to live up to the democratic ideal of informed, dispassionate, and wise citizens, it is not surprising that collective decision-making is often more tolerated than embraced. It is in this context that researchers of public opinion have sought to systematically examine collective opinion to identify the scale of the error and the scope of meaningful attitudes. When trying to reconcile the individual-level shortcomings of the average citizen with the potentially meaningful nature of aggregate opinion, Page and Shapiro (1992), among others, introduced the language of "signal" and "noise." Building on this insight, Erikson, MacKuen, and Stimson (2002) argue for an attentive public (made up of those whose interest in and knowledge about politics bring meaning and order to aggregate opinion) and an inattentive public (with its limited understanding and interest in politics), and it is the inattentive public that introduces errors (the noise). Although I will argue that dividing up the public into two groups—attentive and inattentive—has its limitations, the idea that aggregate opinion contains both signal and noise is an important one. Even under idealized conditions in which the public is comprised of *überrational* individuals, errors are likely introduced into aggregate opinion through sampling error, unrepresentative surveys (possibly due to high turndown rates), news developments while the survey is being conducted, etc. In this case, the errors are likely to be small relative to the signal provided by an informed public. But when issues are only on the political agenda intermittently or novel issues arise on the agenda, the noise in aggregate opinion may be large relative to the signal.

The purpose of this chapter is to more formally assess the "signal" and the "noise" in aggregate opinion using time series techniques that make it possible to determine whether repeated measures of public opinion are plagued by errors or constitute something meaningful. If aggregate opinion is dominated by "errors," then we cannot identify a meaningful signal and the argument for collective rationality is undermined. If, on the other hand, the errors are small relative to the signal, then defenses of the legitimacy of collective opinion carry more weight. This chapter shows that aggregate time series of some common public opinion questions do, in fact, constitute more signal than noise, but casts doubt on current theories as to the source of this signal.

Distinguishing the Signal from the Noise

The terms "signal" and "noise" do have some intuitive meaning as exemplified by the title of Nate Silver's (2012) best-selling book, *The Signal and the Noise*. The signal is conceptualized (not surprisingly) as the meaningful part of a time series. If there is systematic change in a time series, it is possible to detect a signal. On the other hand, if public opinion fluctuates without any clear pattern over time, it is characterized as noise. The term "errors" is used to describe the distance of observed opinion from the signal and noisy time series are usually described as having lots of random errors. So imagine the public is surveyed on an issue that a lot of people don't have a fixed opinion about, like the benefits of a flat tax on income. Some people are likely to say that they are more supportive of a flat tax than they might really be if they were fully informed and others might say they are less supportive than they might be if fully informed. If opinions are measured on this issue repeatedly over time, there are likely to be random swings in the level of support for the issue due to the public's overall uncertainty about its potential costs and benefits. Thus, the time series will likely be a noisy one.

Although the terms signal and noise are commonly used in discussions of public opinion, it is less common to try to estimate the amount of signal and noise. Moving from a general discussion of signal and noise to a more precise estimate does requires some specialized tools and language, and they are described below. The virtue of estimating these precisely is that it is possible to say more than public opinion has a strong signal or is very noisy. With precise estimates, it is possible to find cases in the middle that have a reasonably strong signal, but also are fairly noisy. In addition, precise estimates mean that we can distinguish between issues in terms of their signal and noise and to develop and test theories and hypotheses about which issues are likely to be noisy and which should have a strong signal.

Although there are many tools for distinguishing the signal from the noise in time-series analysis, one common approach is to use state-space modeling and the Kalman filter. The virtue of state-space modeling is that it can provide a clear and intuitive depiction of the signal-to-noise components and this approach is used throughout this chapter. (A more detailed explanation of these models is provided in subsequent chapters.) The essential idea is to estimate the underlying signal in a time series and see how strong the signal is relative to the noise. When aggregate opinion exhibits a lot of random noise, it is difficult to detect the underlying signal. On the other hand, when there is a very strong signal, random errors are relatively small. In a time-series plot, each observation will be very close to the underlying signal and the errors will be difficult to observe visually, but state-space models make it possible to distinguish between them numerically.

Aggregate public opinion is easily represented in the state-space format using two equations:

Measurement equation (or signal + noise): $y_t = x_t + v_t$

Signal equation (or transition equation): $x_t = \phi x_{t-1} + \omega_t$

Observed opinion from a poll is represented as y_t and it contains some random error, v_t. As an example, if the poll were about the public's approval of Congress, y_t would be the percent of a survey that reported approving of the job done by Congress. We know that this will be measured with some error since we are using a sample, rather than surveying the population, and some people will be uncertain about the job that Congress is doing and will under- or over-report their approval. The underlying signal, x_t, is not observed but can be estimated along with its own error component, ω_t and a persistence parameter, ϕ. The underlying signal is a latent variable—that is, there is some core assessment of the job that Congress is doing, but it is difficult to identify given the tools for measurement that must be used (surveys) and the uncertainty that arises from an imperfectly informed public.

The signal-to-noise ratio is a useful way to summarize precisely the characteristics of public opinion collected over time in terms of how much error there is. The signal-to-noise ratio is calculated by taking the variance of the signal error divided by the measurement error, $\sigma_\omega^2 / \sigma_v^2$. When observed opinion is plagued by random errors, the signal-to-noise ratio is small and when the signal variance is strong relative to the error, the signal-to-noise ratio is large. A comparison of time series with varying signal-to-noise ratios is made in Figure 2.1. The signal is the gray line in the time plot.

The low signal-to-noise ratio in the first panel means that the signal is effectively lost in the noise that accompanies it. As the signal-to-noise ratio increases, the signal is easier to detect and the random noise is more difficult to observe. Signal-to-noise ratios that are less than one indicate that the noise is greater than the signal, as shown in the first panel of Figure 2.1. When the signal-to-noise ratio is one, the variances of the noise and signal are exactly matched, as shown in the second panel of Figure 2.1, and signal-to-noise ratios greater than one mean that the series has more signal than noise (the bottom panels of Figure 2.1).

A comparison of two different public opinion series can help illustrate this point. The upper panel of Figure 2.2 shows the percentage of Democrats supporting Barack Obama during the Democratic primary season of 2008, from polls collected by the Gallup organization. The trend in this case is a steady increase in support for Obama with some mild deviations from that trend. In other words, there is a signal from the upward trend, but there is a fair amount of "noise" as the poll tracks his steady increase in support. Since the 2008 primary was dominated by two strong candidates who were quite similar in their policy positions, it is not too surprising that support for Barack Obama is characterized by a modest trend and a fair amount of noise. Although primaries garner a lot of media attention, they do not generate a lot of novel "news" that might produce marked shifts in support. Candidates stick close to their campaign's message and only rarely alter their campaign strategy. What

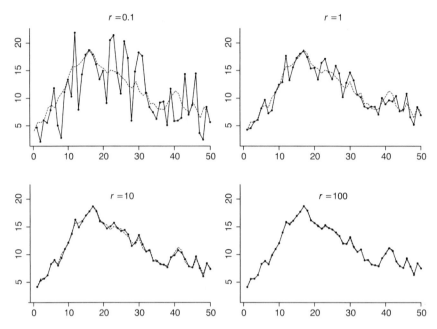

FIGURE 2.1 Simulated time series with varying signal-to-noise ratios, r. The dashed line is the estimate of the signal. Code for figure from Petris and Petrone (2009, 90).

does provide some "signal" is winning primaries and delegates and the steady rise in Obama's support reflects this.

The lower panel of Figure 2.2 shows monthly approval of government policy as reported in the Thomson Reuters/University of Michigan Surveys of Consumers. Respondents are asked, "As to the economic policy of the government—I mean steps taken to fight inflation or unemployment—would you say the government is doing a good job, only fair, or a poor job?" The line in the figure is the signal (rather than a line connecting the points as in most time-series plots). The signal-to-noise ratio for this series is 19/1 and this means that the observed points and the signal remain very close to one another throughout the time period. The series includes boom and bust cycles consistent with the economic cycles experienced by the US economy. In particular, according to the survey, the peak performance by the government in managing the economy occurred at the end of the Clinton administration and fell fairly dramatically starting in 2001. The steady decline continued throughout President George W. Bush's administration, hitting its nadir in 2008. These steady twists and turns are characteristic of series with a strong signal since there is inevitably important "news" or "events" that produce these changes in direction, as opposed to a series with lots of random error where the series drifts away from the signal in a more haphazard pattern.

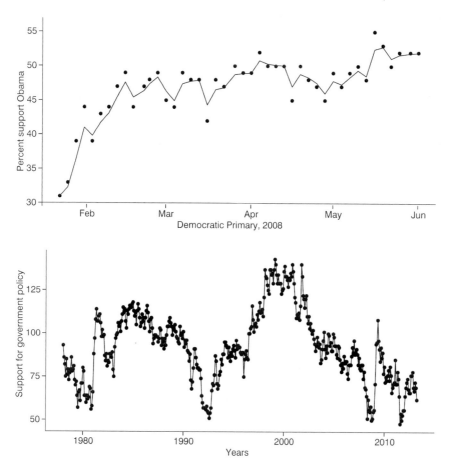

FIGURE 2.2 *Upper panel:* signal and noise for support among Democrats for Barack Obama in the 2008 primary. The signal is the black line, signal-to-noise ratio, 1/1. *Lower panel:* support for the government's economic policy. Signal-to-noise ratio is 19/1.

These two measures of public opinion, support for Barack Obama in the 2008 primary and the public's assessment of government in managing the economy, provide a stark contrast in terms of the certainty in which the public evaluated these issues. Although primaries occur regularly, the candidates running in them shift over time and this introduces a lot of uncertainty into the public's assessment of them, as reflected in the signal-to-noise ratio of one. On the other hand, economic conditions and the role that government plays in managing them are a somewhat more predictable context in which to measure opinion, and this is evident in the high signal-to-noise ratio estimated in the public's assessment of the job that government is doing managing the economy.

Signal and Noise in Key Measures of Aggregate Opinion

By looking across issues, it is possible to gauge more effectively the nature of random error and better understand the conditions under which it might arise. Using cross-sectional data, Althaus (2003, 123) looks at a variety of issues and the extent to which they should be subject to "random information effects" or "systematic information effects," in other words, random error that cancels out or a systematic component such as the signal discussed above. Using this distinction between a random and a systematic component is useful when looking for issues in which to assess the underlying meaning and coherence of public opinion. Althaus studies the policy-approval questions that are routinely used to gauge presidential performance, and these include questions about the president's ability to handle issues like the economy and foreign policy. Althaus assigns these policy-approval questions to the random error category since respondents need to have relatively up-to-date information about the political and economic environment in order to meaningfully answer them and that is challenging for many people. Opinion on these issues seems to contain a detectable amount of noise, or random error. In addition, questions about the president's handling of foreign policy and economic management require respondents to parse their overall assessment of the president into these subcategories. For example, if the news were dominated by economic issues, respondents might have difficulty thinking about key foreign policy successes or failures, leading some people to overestimate and others to underestimate their evaluation of the president in handling foreign policy issues. According to Althaus, the measure of *overall* job approval, by contrast, does not appear to have a lot of random error to it. Partly this might be familiarity with the question, since the presidential-approval question is routinely discussed in the media, and there are plenty of cues that people can reliably draw upon in making this general assessment. Thus, there is less random error when measuring it. The virtues of both the policy-approval and general job-approval questions for studying aggregate opinion is that we expect them to vary in the amount of random error, and they have been asked often enough that they can be studied over time.

In order to assess the random and systematic components of aggregate opinion of the president on overall job approval and on specific policy issues, I rely on multiple indicators of the concepts of interest using data from both Gallup and CBS News. In the case of overall presidential job approval, the Gallup series is sufficiently complete (i.e., there are relatively few months in which no survey questions about the job performance of the president were asked) to use it alone, as is done in many studies. However, using both the CBS and Gallup data provides a way to estimate the reliability of the Gallup survey and to assess random variability in the model.[2] Merging time series using state-space modeling and the Kalman filter is quite straightforward and is described in Jackman (2009) and Shumway and Stoffer (2006).[3] For policy questions about the president's handling of economic and foreign policy issues, the data are less complete and merging information from CBS and Gallup is necessary in order to construct a monthly time series. Merging these time series produces a more consistent estimate of underlying opinion and also allows us to see differences across surveys in the signal-to-noise ratio.[4]

The Kalman filter is well-suited to this task of calculating the amount of random variation that accrues in these evaluations of presidential performance. Through estimation of the transition and measurement equations, we get an estimate of σ_ε^2 the random error in the observed survey data.[5]

Estimates from the Kalman filter for presidential job approval show that the signal is quite strong.[6] The error variances of both approval series are quite small relative to the overall movement in the series, leading to quite high signal-to-noise ratios for both series, 2.16 for CBS and 7.5 for Gallup.[7] The estimate of the noise variance, σ_v^2, for Gallup (1.82) is less than that CBS (6.32), and this indicates the Gallup series is less influenced by random noise than the CBS series. It is important to note that the signal-to-noise ratios are not the same despite the similar sample sizes used by the two survey organizations.[8] If sampling error were the only contributor to random error, the error variances for the two indicators would be nearly identical.

The reliability of the two indicators can be calculated from the squared correlation of the CBS and Gallup series with the underlying signal (which is estimated from the data). The correspondence between the signal and the Gallup series is very strong, with an estimated correlation between the observed data and the signal of 0.99 and a reliability estimate of 0.99. For CBS, the correlation between the signal and the observed data is 0.97, producing a reliability estimate of 0.96. The high measures of reliability provide additional evidence that these measures contain little random error. The estimate of the lagged, latent opinion (ϕ) is 0.95, indicating that there is a high degree of persistence in the public's evaluation of the president. The results of this analysis confirm that on a relatively general question like approval of the president, the public provides a consistent signal.

This issue of the signal and noise in public opinion can be further examined by looking at questions about policy approval. I begin with an estimate of the signal and noise in economic approval.[9] To measure economic approval, respondents in surveys are asked if they "approve of the job that the president is doing managing the economy." For economic approval, the estimates of noise are much greater than in overall job approval. Comparing economic approval to job approval, the variance in the signal is smaller (8.81 to 13.67) while the noise variances for the Gallup and CBS polls are both larger. For CBS, the random error variance increases from 6.32 to 8.58, and for Gallup, the increase is from

1.82 to 6.24. The signal-to-noise ratios are appreciably smaller for economic approval. For both the Gallup and CBS surveys, the signal-to-noise ratio was about 1, meaning that there was nearly as much noise as signal. The estimate of the lagged latent variable is 0.97, indicating that as with job approval, the public's evaluation of the president this month will be quite similar to last month's, once the random noise is accounted for. Overall, the signal that the public provides about the president's handling of the economy is much weaker than the one for its evaluation of the president's job approval. One explanation for this might be that people feel that they need to base their answer to the economic approval question more on economic conditions, and their ability to link economic conditions to the president is less reliable than simply keeping a running tally of their view of the president's overall job performance.

Foreign policy is a challenging issue on which to study the signal and noise in public opinion since foreign policy, almost by its very nature, is an area in which the public must rethink and reevaluate its views. There are ongoing issues that influence the public's evaluation of the president like the Cold War and the war on terrorism, but in the midst of these are foreign policy events in relatively unfamiliar areas of the world like Panama, Lebanon, or Somalia. So in order to make a decision about presidential performance on foreign policy, both familiar and unfamiliar information must be processed. Because of this we should expect both a high degree of variation in the signal and a good deal of noise in the public's evaluation of the president in managing foreign policy. The variance in the systematic component (the signal) is 12.77 which is close to the value of 13.67 for overall approval.[10] The random noise variation for the CBS and Gallup measures are much bigger, however. The variance for CBS is 14.48 and for Gallup it is 10.46. This leads to a signal-to-noise ratio that is again close to 1 as in the case of economic approval. The effect of the previous month's foreign policy is fairly persistent with an estimate of ϕ that is 0.95. Overall, the public's evaluation of the president on foreign policy varies considerably over time, much of this due to the influence of rallying events like the Gulf War and 9/11. Such large shifts are usually evidence of a strong signal, but in this case, these large structural shifts are accompanied by quite a bit of random error as well.

Figure 2.3 shows the estimate of the signal for foreign policy approval and includes estimates of the standard error bounds around the estimate. In the upper panel of the figure, the time series plot shows much more noise in the data than was evident in the question about the public's support for the government's economic policy (Figure 2.2, lower panel). With this much noise, one concern might be that it is impossible to distinguish any meaningful differences in foreign policy approval over time. The standard error bars can help address this since they can be used to see whether opinion at the high and low points in the series are significantly different from each other. For foreign policy, the lowest

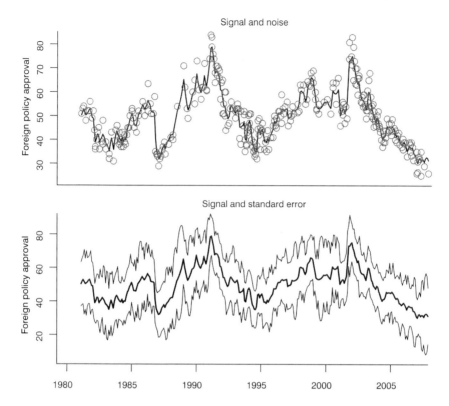

FIGURE 2.3 Foreign policy approval Gallup and CBS Data, 1981 to 2007. Lower panel: wide line is the signal, thin lines represent the standard errors.

estimate is for George W. Bush in 2007 (28.5±25) and the highest is for George H.W. Bush in February 1991 (79±15). The confidence intervals for these data points do not overlap (the high estimate for 2007 is 53.5 percent and the low estimate for 1991 is 64 percent). Therefore, even though there is a high degree of noise, we see significant differences across time, indicating that the signal is identifiable. But it is clear that for researchers, there is a lot more uncertainty about the signal for foreign policy than for presidential job approval.

If presidential job approval is a relatively "easy" judgment for the public (using the terminology of Carmines and Stimson [1989]), then assessing the current condition of the national economy is a more challenging one. Given that there is objective information about the state of the economy available for citizens to acquire and process, we might expect a greater degree of random errors on this issue. Noise might arise from the fact that all this information is partially processed by citizens, and some people are moved to view the economy positively because of one set of indicators while others might view it more pessimistically in response to a different set of indicators. Those who are

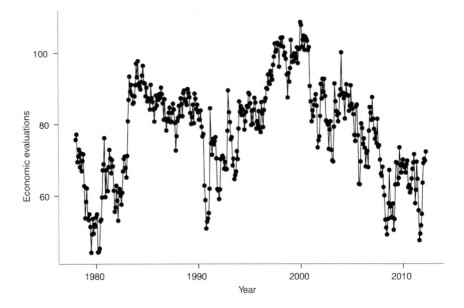

FIGURE 2.4 Signal and noise model for consumer sentiment, signal plus noise, 1978 to 2012.

attentive to the news might register quite different opinions than those who are inattentive, providing additional opportunity for noise to creep in. Conversely, however, researchers have found that often the public can follow economic trends fairly closely by relying on information in the environment. The idea is that there is enough information about economic conditions in the typical person's environment (gas prices, food prices, stories about people getting hired or laid off) that they can make a good assessment of economic conditions (Haller & Norpoth 1997). In this view, with the necessary information for people to make judgments about the economy readily available, the amount of noise in economic assessments should be relatively small.

I turn next to the public's assessment of economic conditions using the Consumer Sentiment Index that is part of the University of Michigan's Surveys of Consumers. Figure 2.4 shows the signal and noise for the public's evaluation of the economy. The public's overall assessment, as captured by the signal, closely follows objective economic conditions during this time period. The public's perceptions of economic conditions during the start of the Reagan administration were generally pessimistic, but the public rated the economy better as economic conditions improved. Evaluations of the economy fell to a new low during the latter part of the George H.W. Bush administration, but then rebounded during the historic economic growth under President Bill Clinton's watch. The public became more pessimistic about economic conditions in the wake of the terrorist attacks in September 2001, recovered to some extent, and then diminished again during the economic crises at the end of George W. Bush's administration.

Despite the complexity of economic evaluations and the potential for random error to occur, a strong signal emerges with a signal-to-noise ratio of 24/1. Figure 2.4 includes the signal and the observed values for consumer sentiment. As with presidential job approval, the signal is so strong that it is difficult to detect the errors in the figure. In other words, observed opinion is very close to the underlying signal and the random errors that do arise are quite small relative to the movement in consumer sentiment. Citizens do seem to have enough information about economic conditions to make consistent assessments of the economy. (The extent to which these are "good" evaluations will be assessed in Chapter 6.)

On the whole, this examination of the signal-to-noise ratio provides evidence that aggregate public opinion has some degree of coherence to it, but that the amount of coherence (or signal) can vary by issue, with the policy questions like the performance of the president in managing foreign affairs and the economy exhibiting more random error than the more familiar evaluations of presidential approval and economic conditions. In none of these issues, however, does the noise completely drown out the signal. This might not be true when looking at issues that only get onto the political agenda periodically and at times of crisis, like the regulation of finance. Druckman and Leeper (2012) emphasize the importance of "stability" as a desirable characteristic of public opinion, noting that it is often lacking in studies of individual-level opinion, but as shown here, is evident in macro-level studies. And with the precise estimates of the signal-to-noise ratio, it is possible to confirm that issues like presidential approval and assessments of the economy have this stability and ones like evaluations of the performance of the president in managing the economy and foreign policy have less (although it is not missing entirely). The analysis undertaken so far is also consistent with the argument of Page and Shapiro (1992) in which they contend that a coherent signal arises amidst the modest and random errors of the uninformed. The analysis is a partial confirmation of their view of the "rational" public since public opinion does move with enough consistency or signal that it appears to be meaningful. In the next section, we turn to the question of whether the signal is in fact a byproduct of the attentive public.

Do High-Information Citizens Produce this Signal?

For those who study collective political rationality, the source of the signal that brings meaning and coherence to a large-scale democracy like ours is the "attentive public." Despite the fact that many, if not most, people fail to meet the standards of the ideal citizen, some people do come closer than others, and it is these people (presumably a lot like the ones reading this book) who we have to thank for the legitimacy of the political system. Citizens who possess a good understanding of the institutions of government, a knowledge of the key players, a familiarity with issues on the political agenda, and access to changing news bring consistency and rationality to public opinion and the political system by updating their opinions in systematic fashion. This idea of the attentive public is appealing and provides a satisfying remedy to the problem of the inattentive public. But does the world divide so nicely into an attentive and inattentive public and are the effects of the inattentive public so innocuous as to conveniently disappear upon aggregation?

Is There an Attentive Public in Aggregate Opinion?

In order to assess the role of the attentive public in bringing order and stability to collective opinion, it is necessary to try to identify those people who consistently follow political events and news reports and systematically evaluate them in order to update their opinion. Finding meaningful measures of political knowledge and sophistication continues to vex those who study public opinion using cross-sectional data even though there are survey questions that try to assess these concepts.[11] The goal is to find measures that can distinguish those who have the interest, information, and knowledge to translate changes in the environment into meaningful public opinion, but it is difficult to easily identify the questions and sources of information that distinguish the informed from the uninformed.[12] These tasks do not get any easier when moving to the aggregate level where our measures of political knowledge are much more limited.

Thus, in order to gain some potential insight into the behavior of the politically informed, I rely on measures of education. As a proxy for political knowledge and information, education is admittedly crude. However, despite its limitations, education continues to be an important variable for understanding political behavior and can provide a general sense of the differences in political sophistication and knowledge. (See for examples of the use of education as a measure of knowledge, Converse [1964], MacKuen [1984], Krause [1997], Krause and Granato [1998]). We do know that higher levels of education are correlated with a better understanding of political institutions, and so on.

Fortunately, Gallup and some of the polls sponsored by the media, like CBS and ABC, do ask respondents about their level of education and these can be used to disaggregate opinion across levels of education. I begin with a comparison of differences in political information by comparing three subgroups, those with a high school diploma, some college, and a college degree.

According to the prevailing theory of collective rationality (Page & Shapiro 1992, Erikson, MacKuen & Stimson 2002), groups with higher levels of information should have a stronger signal and less noise than people with lower levels of education—that is, we would expect a greater degree of random noise among those with less education and also a signal that is not as consistent or fails to follow precisely the same patterns as higher education groups. I use two data sets to examine the behavior of high, medium, and low education groups over time: 1. the Gallup presidential job approval series and 2. the public's rating of current economic conditions, using data from CBS, ABC, and Gallup. These two issues are different from one another in a way that is useful for generalizing beyond these specific cases. The presidential approval series is useful for understanding political behavior on a issue that has the potential to be highly partisan. The rating of the economy is an issue that is not on its surface as partisan, and is at times referred to as an "objective" question (Bartels 1996).

When looking over time at presidential approval by education group (high school, some college, college graduate), the surprising finding is that the series are nearly indistinguishable from each other.[13] In addition, the series do not show that those with a college degree provide a stronger or more consistent signal that than those without one.

To examine this more systematically, I correlate the three education series with overall approval (analysis not shown). All the series grouped by education have a strong correlation with overall approval, but the strongest relationship with overall approval is the measure of approval for high school graduates—those thought to have the lowest amount of political information. This is a surprising finding, one that is essentially the opposite of what Page and Shapiro's analysis suggests. Following their logic, we would assume that the presidential approval series would be dominated by the views of those with higher levels of information and attention to politics.

To further assess the impact of education on aggregate opinion, we can compare the signal-to-noise ratios across these groups. Since these estimates are based on a subset of the full sample, the signal-to-noise ratios are lower than those estimated for approval, but they are quite consistent across educational groups for presidential approval. The signal-to-noise ratio is highest for college graduates, 5.45, but this is only a little higher than that for high school graduates and those with some college, both of which were about 4.0. For each of the educational categories, the signal-to-noise ratio is greater than 1, indicating that there is more signal than noise. The key point, however, is that the noise does not markedly decrease as the level of education increases.

The public's assessment of economic conditions provides an opportunity to further examine this issue of the role of education in aggregate opinion. Since this a judgment about economic conditions, it is possible that those with higher education more readily process economic information and reduce the amount of noise in their assessment of the economy compared to those with the lowest levels of education. But, as noted above, "byproduct" theory suggests that enough information about economic conditions reaches those even with the lowest understanding of political and economic issues, and if this is true, there may not be much difference across education groups.

Because there is not a single survey organization that asked the same question consistently enough to construct a monthly measure, I use data from three different survey organizations-CBS, ABC, and Gallup.[14] The correlations among the series for rating the economy by educational group are very high when the variables are correlated in their levels and after differencing. For the variables in their levels, the correlations are all above 0.95 and when differenced the lowest correlation (0.78) is between some college and college graduate (0.94). Clearly, there is no obvious case to be made that those with higher levels of information differ from those with less. Overall, it is not possible to make a strong case that information or education is the factor that brings order and meaning to aggregate public opinion. Looking broadly at the way that education differences in the population might influence aggregate opinion, there is reason to believe that those with higher levels of education have more knowledge, but little reason to believe that they process new information any differently than those with lower levels of education or knowledge. Thus, if there is a "miracle of aggregation," it does not appear that knowledge or education are the source of this miracle.

Party by Education

In order to investigate further the sources of the signal in aggregate public opinion, the data are disaggregated by party and education. Figure 2.5 shows the time plot of these disaggregated series for ratings of the economy.[15] The figure confirms that the signal is defined by party not by education. This is evident from the fact that each of the panels looks nearly identical. If education were the dominant subgroup, differences across groups would be evident.[16]

This finding is corroborated by looking at correlations by subgroup, as reported in Table 2.1. The lower half of the correlation table shows the correlations for the change in the variables (differenced) and the upper triangle shows the correlations in their level. It is clear from the table that the correlations in the variables in their level are stronger than the change in the variables. This indicates that the data trend together and that the trends among partisan groups are quite strong. The correlations within the partisan groups for variables at their level are quite strong, with both Democrats and Republicans correlated at greater than 0.94. (These are marked in bold in the table.) The correlation among the education groups fall off sharply when compared to the party groups. When looking at the change in the variables (lower part of the table), the same general pattern appears, although not quite as dramatically as when looking at the levels. Within the Democratic partisans, the correlations range from 0.56 to 0.65, and for Republicans the correlation within the group, the correlations are

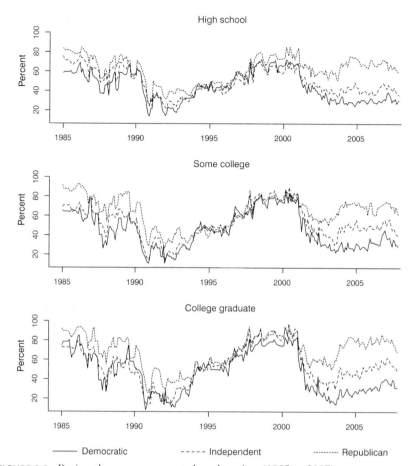

FIGURE 2.5   Rating the economy, party by education (1985 to 2007)

in the middle to high sixties, 0.65 to 0.69. There are a few correlations within the education groups that are quite high. For example, there is a correlation of 0.76 between Independents with only a high school education and Democrats with a only high school education. Overall, the correlations confirm the pattern that has emerged from looking at the disaggregated data: party seems to matter more than knowledge in providing structure to aggregate time series.

Who Provides the Signal? An Alternative Explanation and Evidence

The analysis above draws into question the claim that it is those with the most knowledge who are responsible for the order that we observe in aggregate public opinion.

TABLE 2.1 Monthly correlations for economic evaluations between education and partisan groups, 1985–2007

	Dem High school	Dem Some college	Dem College graduate	Ind High school	Ind Some college	Ind College graduate	Rep High school	Rep Some college	Rep College graduate
Dem High school	1.0	**0.94**	**0.94**	0.89	0.87	0.85	0.63	0.65	0.65
Dem Some college	**0.57**	1.0	**0.96**	0.84	0.92	0.92	0.63	0.63	0.68
Dem College graduate	**0.56**	**0.65**	1.0	0.86	0.88	0.90	0.61	0.64	0.68
Ind High school	0.76	0.54	0.54	1.0	**0.87**	**0.80**	0.83	0.86	0.80
Ind Some college	0.55	0.65	0.56	**0.56**	1.0	**0.95**	0.82	0.81	0.86
Ind College graduate	0.48	0.54	0.56	**0.57**	**0.62**	1.0	0.74	0.73	0.83
Rep High school	0.59	0.45	0.46	0.69	0.50	0.53	1.0	**0.96**	**0.94**
Rep Some college	0.53	0.42	0.46	0.64	0.46	0.52	**0.66**	1.0	**0.94**
Rep College graduate	0.49	0.36	0.47	0.62	0.45	0.62	**0.69**	**0.65**	1.0

$n = 275$

The upper half of the matrix (shaded) are correlations in their levels, and the lower half when the variables are differenced.

Key within-party correlations are in bold.

Experimental studies of individual political decision-making argue that this search for exceptional citizens who conform to the archetype of the rational citizen is misguided. The experiments show that few people make decisions in a coolly rational, cost-benefit mode and that inevitably decisions get made, even among the most politically attentive, through the use of information shortcuts or heuristics. The model citizen is nowhere to be found.

An innovative study by Lau and Redlawsk (2006) sheds light on one source of stability: partisanship. In their analysis, Lau and Redlawsk use an experiment to study what type of decision-making might lead to "correct voting." Correct voting is operationalized in an experiment as the degree to which voters are satisfied with their choice afterwards. What they find is that people who rely on partisanship and heuristics rather than rational decision-making have the highest rate of correct voting. Thus, their study suggests that it is partisans who reduce errors in aggregate public opinion rather than the attentive public.

In his analysis of partisan updating, Bartels (2002) provides additional insight into this question about the relative role of party and information in opinion change. In his analysis, he uses panel data to look at opinion change on a host of issues—from respondents' views about the personal characteristics of presidents to their views of the economy—and shows clear evidence of partisan bias as individuals update their views, regardless of whether the issue is valence or evaluative. But because the panel data includes measures of the political knowledge of respondents (something not directly measurable in aggregate time series), he can more effectively compare the relative impact of information and party. The results of this part of Bartels' analysis provide clear corroborating evidence for the decisive role of party and the limited influence of information in updating behavior across nearly all the issues. He finds that the differences between high information and low information respondents in their updating are insignificant. Thus, the panel data predict a pattern over time that is similar to the one shown in Figure 2.5.

In order to examine more fully the relationship between knowledge and party, I use NES survey data from the 2004 elections to show how error rates among citizens would change as we move from an attentive to an inattentive public in a manner described by Bartels (1996) and used by Althaus (1998, 2003). However, I add an additional component to this analysis, and that is partisanship. The basic procedure used by Bartels and Althaus is to estimate a regression model, predicting opinion with an exhaustive set of demographic variables and an index of political knowledge constructed from questions in the survey. The model includes interaction terms between each of the demographic variables and the knowledge question. Once this model is estimated, the parameter estimates are used to calculate "informed" public opinion by resetting the knowledge variable to its highest value. This simulates how public opinion would look if all the voters were high information but had their specific demographic characteristics. We can use these estimates as a basis of comparison to see, for example, how they compare to actual opinion.[17] I use these calculations of informed opinion and simulate the errors that would arise if the level of information for the public as a whole changed from high to low. The error rates for both presidential approval and economic conditions are shown in Figure 2.6. The horizontal axis represents the political knowledge variable and the vertical axis shows the estimated average error for each issue. For presidential approval, the straight dashed line in the lower panel of Figure 2.6 is the estimated root mean squared error (RMSE) from the difference between informed opinion and less than fully informed opinion. In the simulation, the knowledge variable varies from a high of 10 to a low of 1. Thus a higher RMSE means that the errors that the public makes in comparison to informed opinion are larger. The fact that the RMSE rises as knowledge declines is what we would expect—a more knowledgeable public makes smaller errors than one low in knowledge.

In order to assess the role of partisanship, I add in partisanship as an explanatory factor in estimating opinion. The curved line on the graph is the change in the error (RMSE) as the level of knowledge changes with partisanship included. As the graph shows, the flattening of the line indicates that partisanship leads to smaller errors for an ill-informed public and larger errors for an informed public. For presidential approval, the reduction of errors associated with partisanship is more dramatic for those with lower knowledge. This finding is consistent with the idea that the more informed public is also highly partisan, so partisan that it introduces errors in their opinion. On the other hand, those on the lower end of the knowledge rating benefit from partisanship, making their opinion closer to "informed opinion."

The analysis for the public's evaluation of the economy is reported in the upper panel of Figure 2.6. In this case, the public is asked whether they think that economic conditions are getting worse. Here we see the same pattern. The dashed line is relatively straight and falling, and this shows that those who are more knowledgeable about politics make smaller errors overall (i.e, smaller RMSEs). As in the analysis of presidential approval when partisanship is added as an explanatory factor (represented by the solid line in the graph), the errors of the informed public get bigger and those of the uninformed public get smaller.

This is an important finding, since it demonstrates that partisanship can play two roles simultaneously. For those with low information, party cues can provide a much-needed road map between information in the political and economic environment and expressed opinion. For those who are already fairly well-informed, the impact of partisanship is more complex. Those who are more informed also tend to be highly partisan and so there is a complex interaction between the two. The consequence of this might be to make those who are most informed more error-prone than they might otherwise be, and

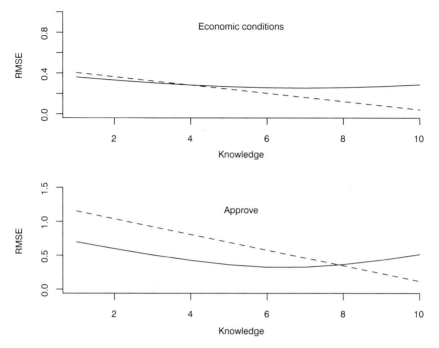

FIGURE 2.6 Errors (RMSE) for presidential approval and economic evaluations and informed opinion, varying knowledge and partisanship

the errors are likely to be systematic rather than random since people from the same party will likely make the same errors.

As reported in *The New York Times*, a recent Pew Study on climate change provides a concrete example of how partisanship and education can interact (Lapidos 2013). When asked about the human contribution to climate change, there is a 29 percentage point difference between college-educated and non-college educated Democrats on the issue, with 86 percent of college-educated Democrats agreeing that human activity contributes to climate change, while 57 percent of those with less than a college diploma agree. For Republicans, there is only a 5 percentage point difference between college-educated Republicans (28 percent agree that human activity contributes to climate change) and those Republicans without a college degree (23 percent agree). The explanation offered by Michael Dimock of the Pew Research Center is that when Democrats go to college and learn scientific information about the impact of human activity on climate change, they get a message that is consistent with what they are hearing from leaders of their party (Lapidos 2013). College-educated Republicans, on the other hand, are likely to learn about the scientific consensus on the impact of humans on the climate, but this is at odds with the information that they are hearing from Republican leaders. As a result, the party cues trump the educational effects and make college-educated Republicans think about issues like climate change in ways that are strikingly close to those without a college degree.

Conclusion

The results of this analysis provide some insight into the nature of collective political rationality. The findings are consistent with the argument made by Page and Shapiro in their defense of aggregate political rationality. The public does appear to update its opinion in a manner consistent with their conceptualization of collective rationality. Aggregate public opinion is comprised of both signal and error. As was shown here, the ratio of signal to error can vary across issues, with "easy" issues like approval or disapproval of the president showing a high degree of signal and more difficult issues like foreign policy having a higher degree of error. But, in both cases, there is a signal that is still meaningful.

The analysis here provides more precise evidence about the nature of the signal and noise. By specifically modeling the signal and noise across a variety of issues, it is possible to say more explicitly what part of aggregate opinion is a meaningful signal and what part can be considered random noise. In addition, by differentiating the amount of signal and noise in aggregate opinion, we can begin to better understand why some issues are plagued by noise and others have a strong signal.

What is important about the analysis in this chapter is that the consistency that we observe in aggregate opinion does not appear to be the result of an attentive public compensating for the foibles of an inattentive one. The structure of aggregate opinion seems to be more defined by the effects of partisanship than education. This is evident by examining data disaggregated by partisanship and education and observing that opinion is clustered predominantly by party and not at all by education. Looking in depth more at knowledge effects using cross-sectional data yields a similar finding. Partisanship dominates information differences. Thus, understanding collective political rationality requires moving beyond the "miracle of aggregation" and looking instead for the complex ways in which partisanship brings coherence to aggregate public opinion.

Appendix: A Formal Description of Signal and Noise

The following is a more formal description of the updating model that can be used to investigate signal and noise. The basic premise, as derived from the "miracle of aggregation" is that when public opinion is observed y_t contains both a systematic component, x_t and a random error component ω_t. The idea of random error in surveys is a familiar one, but the focus is generally on sampling error which is simply the uncertainty of trying to use a sample to generalize about a population. But, the argument made by advocates of the rational public is that the error in surveys is more than simple sampling error since it can arise from incomplete information, data collection errors, "top of the head sampling" (Zaller 1992), ambivalence (Feldman & Zaller 1992, Alvarez & Brehm 2002), or time elapsed from key events. But the key assumption is that these errors are random.

This approach can be summarized by describing the measurement and transition equations using terminology from state space-modeling. The measurement equation contains the measurement error v_t and can be used to calculate its variance, σ_v^2, while the transition equation describes the dynamics of the signal and can be used to capture its variance, σ_ω^2.

Measurement equation $y_t = x_t + v_t$

Transition equation $x_t = \phi x_{t-i} + \omega_t$

In the transition equation, which charts the path of the signal or opinion without random error, opinion changes in relation to past opinion as indicated by the lagged value of x_t. How the past influences the present is also guided by ϕ. When ϕ is zero, the past matters not at all and opinion can swing widely from one time period to another (i.e., the public has no memory of where it was before). Alternatively, when ϕ is 1, the past observations are fully felt in the present (i.e., there is full memory of the past). Values of ϕ between 0 and 1 imply some middle ground. The public does not veer from the past in wild swings, but neither is current opinion entirely a function of past opinion.[18]

The Kalman filter provides a way to estimate the relationship between observed opinion and the unobserved signal.

The updating equations for the filter are:

$$x_t = \phi x_{t-1} + K_t(y_t - \phi x_{t-1})$$

where

$$K_t = \frac{P_{t-1} + \sigma_\omega^2}{(P_{t-1} + \sigma_\omega^2) + \sigma_v^2}$$

In the updating equation, changes to underlying opinion will be the byproduct of past opinion and new information captured in the prediction error, $y_t - \phi x_{t-1}$. In the prediction error, a larger gap between what was expected, ϕx_t, and what occurred, y_t, is evidence that measured opinion was different than expected. The question is whether the difference between expected and measured opinion signals a real change in public opinion or whether it is simply noise. In the Bayesian updating model, a change in opinion, as measured by the prediction error, is weighed by K, the Kalman gain. The Kalman gain is a way to keep track of whether opinion is stable or fluctuating.

This model provides a close fit to the problem at hand. For example, if there were a dramatic change in the political or economic environment like a sudden spike in oil prices during a time when opinion was changing very little (i.e., there were fairly calm economic conditions), citizens might see this as a temporary condition and not change their assessment of the economy. On the other hand, during a periods of economic uncertainty, as in September 2008, when in the same week, there were positive reactions to the news that the federal government was going to provide an $85 billion loan to American Insurance Group (AIG) and a negative reaction to the bankruptcy of Lehman Brothers.

The variance term σ_ω^2 represents the error variance in the signal that the public provides regarding particular issues, and σ_v^2 is a measure of noise or randomness in measured opinion. The signal is provided by the informed public who follow issues and update their opinions in response to new information. The ratio of these variances is described as the signal-to-noise ratio. This ratio provides a way to distinguishes issues base on the amount of measurement error and structural error. Issues in which public opinion is weakly formed will have a low signal-to-noise ratio, and ones in which the public has well-formed views will have a high signal-to-noise ratio.[19]

Notes

1. For example, a 2013 poll by the Kaiser Family Foundation estimated that Americans, on average, believe that 28 percent of the federal budget goes to foreign aid when in reality foreign aid constitutes about 1 percent of the federal budget (Brodie, Hamel & Hanna 2013).
2. Estimating the reliability of the Gallup survey is the key here, since it is the most commonly cited measure of presidential approval.
3. The programs used to estimate the merged time series are from Shumway and Stoffer (2006).
4. It is important to note that in merging the data, I use data from the CBS and Gallup separately. In other words, I don't fill in missing values in one series with data from the other. For months in which Gallup or CBS did not conduct a survey, the month is recorded as having missing data. The Kalman filter provides estimates of the underlying signal, despite missing data.
5. The assumption in this model is that the impact of random error will be in the current time period, producing a moving-average (MA) error in the updating model. It is possible to use an estimate of the sampling error in the estimation of the model, as is done by Green, Gerber, and De Boef (1999). However, this assumes that all the error in the survey data is due to sampling and that is not consistent with the theory of aggregate rationality outlined by Page and Shapiro (1992) and others. The random error in measured opinion is also due to the limited knowledge, ambivalence, and inattention of some respondents.
6. The estimates are reported in tabular form in the online supplement at http://gemcavoy.wp.uncg.edu/.
7. The estimate of the Gallup series alone leads to an even higher signal-to-noise ratio, but the point of this analysis is to use data from the two surveys in order to estimate their reliability.

8. Both organizations use a sample size of about 1000 in non-election years and will occasionally use larger samples for surveys conducted in election years.

9. The estimate of the underlying signal and the survey estimates from CBS and Gallup are available in the online supplement http://gemcavoy.wp.uncg.edu/. A figure of the signal and noise is included there as well.

10. The results are available in the online supplement at http://gemcavoy.wp.uncg.edu/.

11. See for example, Bartels (1996, 2002), Delli Carpini and Keeter (1996), and Zaller (1992).

12. Erikson, MacKuen, and Stimson (2002) address this issue in a limited way using GSS questions over time disaggregated by education.

13. The three groups track each other so closely that a graph of them is not particularly useful. But for those who want to see for themselves, the figure is available in the online supplement http://gemcavoy.wp.uncg.edu/. But the lesson is, if you know the trend for one group, you know it for the others as well.

14. As before, the procedure for merging these time series using the Kalman filter is described in Jackman (2009) and Shumway and Stoffer (2006).

15. Both job approval and economic approval of the president show this same pattern: the series are more easily distinguished by party than education. For further examination of the disaggregated series for the economic approval of the president, see McAvoy and Enns (2010).

16. For this analysis of citizens' evaluation of economic conditions, I rely on questions asked primarily by Gallup and CBS news (see online supplement at http://gemcavoy.wp.uncg.edu/ for the actual question wording), but also ABC News. ABC asked about the economy more consistently than the others during the 1980s and makes it possible to study this issue from 1981 to the present, spanning the full terms of four presidents. A similar analysis was conducted using the Index of Consumer Sentiment from the Surveys of Consumers conducted by the University of Michigan. The results of the analysis using the survey questions from CBS, ABC, and Gallup are nearly identical to the analysis of the Index of Consumer Sentiment. I present the data from the combined survey because it can be disaggregated by party and education, and I rely on this disaggregated data in subsequent analyses. The basic task is for respondents to say whether they think that economic conditions are getting better, staying the same, or getting worse.

17. This comparison is what Bartels and Althaus do in their analyses and they find that the actual and informed opinion differ on many issues. Thus, if the public were better informed, opinion would be different and, from their perspective, better.

18. When we look at the role of partisanship in collective public opinion in Chapter 3, a more substantive interpretation of ϕ is developed.

19. This ratio is used extensively in state-space modeling and estimation of the Kalman filter, and within political science is utilized in Green, Gerber, and De Boef (1999) and Green, Palmquist, and Schickler (2002).

Bibliography

Althaus, Scott L. 1998. "Information Effects in Collective Preferences." *American Political Science Review* 92(3):545–558.

Althaus, Scott L. 2003. *Collective Preferences in Democratic Politics.* Cambridge: Cambridge University Press.

Alvarez, R. Michael & John Brehm. 2002. *Hard Choices, Easy Answers*. Princeton, NJ: Princeton University Press.

Bartels, Larry. 1996. "Uninformed Voters: Information Effects in Presidential Elections." *American Journal of Political Science* 40(1):194–230.

Bartels, Larry. 2002. "Beyond the Running Tally: Partisan Bias in Political Perceptions." *Political Behavior* 24(2):117–150.

Brodie, Mollyann, Liz Hamel & Becky Hanna. 2013. *2013 Survey of Americans on the U.S. Role in Global Health*. Memo Park, CA: Kaiser Family Foundation.

Carmines, Edward G. & James A. Stimson. 1989. *Issue Evolution: Race and the Transformation of American Politics*. Princeton, NJ: Princeton University Press.

Converse, Philip E. 1964. "The Nature of Belief Systems in Mass Publics." In David E. Apter (ed), *Ideology and Discontent*. Ann Arbor, MI: University of Michigan Press.

Delli Carpini, Michael X. & Scott Keeter. 1996. *What Americans Know About Politics and Why it Matters*. New Haven, CT: Yale University Press.

Druckman, James N. & Thomas J. Leeper. 2012. "Is Public Opinion Stable? Resolving the Micro/Macro Disconnect in Studies of Public Opinion." *Daedalus* 141(4):50–68.

Erikson, Robert S., Michael B. MacKuen & James A. Stimson. 2002. *The Macro Polity*. New York: Cambridge University Press.

Feldman, Stanley & John R. Zaller. 1992. "The Political Culture of Ambivalence: Ideological Responses to the Welfare State." *American Journal of Political Science* 36(3):268–307.

Green, Donald, Bradley Palmquist & Eric Schickler. 2002. *Partisan Hearts and Minds: Political Parties and the Social Identities of Voters*. New Haven, CT.: Yale University Press.

Green, Donald P., Alan S. Gerber & Suzanna L De Boef. 1999. "Tracking Opinion Over Time: A Method For Reducing Sampling Error." *Public Opinion Quarterly* 63(2):178–192.

Haller, H. Brandon & Helmut Norpoth. 1997. "Reality Bites: News Exposure and Economic Opinion." *Public Opinion Quarterly* 61(4):555–575.

Jackman, Simon. 2009. *Bayesian Analysis for the Social Sciences*. Chichester: Wiley.

Krause, George A. 1997. "Voters, Information Heterogeneity, and the Dynamics of Aggregate Economic Expectations." *American Journal of Political Science* 41(4):1170–1200.

Krause, George A. & Jim Granato. 1998. "Fooling Some of the People Some of the Time? A Test of Weak Rationality with Heterogeneous Information Levels." *Public Opinion Quarterly* 62(2):135–151.

Lapidos, Juliet. 2013. "Global Warming, College, and Partisanship." *The New York Times*, November 13. http://takingnote.blogs.nytimes.com/2013/11/13/global-warming-college-and-partisanship, accessed October 20, 2104

Lau, Richard R. & David P. Redlawsk. 2006. *How Voters Decide: Information Processing during Election Campaigns*. Cambridge: Cambridge University Press.

MacKuen, Michael. 1984. "Exposure to Information, Belief Integration, and Individual Responsiveness to Agenda Change." *American Political Science Review* 78(2):372–391.

McAvoy, Gregory E. & Peter K. Enns. 2010. "Using Approval of the President's Handling of the Economy to Understand Who Polarizes and Why." *Presidential Studies Quarterly* 40(3):545–558.

Page, Benjamin I. & Robert Y. Shapiro. 1992. *The Rational Public: Fifty Years of Trends in Americans' Policy Preferences*. Chicago, IL: University of Chicago Press.

Petris, Giovanni & Sonia Petrone. 2009. *Dynamic Linear Models With R*. New York: Springer-Verlag.

Shumway, Robert H. & David S. Stoffer. 2006. *Time Series Analysis and Its Applications: With R Examples*. New York: Springer.

Silver, Nate. 2012. *The Signal and the Noise: Why So Many Predictions Fail but Some Don't*. New York: Penguin Press.

Surowieki, James. 2005. *The Wisdom of Crowds*. New York: Doubleday.

Zaller, John R. 1992. *The Nature and Origins of Mass Opinion*. New York: Cambridge University Press.

3

THE PARTISAN SIGNAL

In individual-level studies of public opinion, no argument about the importance of partisanship is needed since nearly every study includes some measure of partisanship and inevitably finds that it plays a significant role. As Stokes (1966, 127) notes:

> for most people the tie between party identification and voting behavior involves subtle processes of perceptual adjustment by which the individual assembles an image of current politics consistent with his partisan allegiance.

Experimental studies also suggest that individuals' motivations to maintain consistent attitudes produce strong partisan effects (Gaines et al. 2007, Taber & Lodge 2006). According to individual-level analyses, partisanship influences what information individuals encounter, whether they accept or discount the information, and how they interpret it. In his extensive analysis of panel data on the role of partisanship in opinion, Bartels (2002, 138) summarizes, "Partisan bias in political perceptions plays a crucial role in perpetuating and reinforcing sharp differences in opinion between Democrats and Republicans."

Yet, how individual-level partisanship influences aggregate public opinion remains unclear. Most over-time studies of public opinion evaluate the public as a whole, minimizing or ignoring differences in opinion among partisan loyalists (e.g., MacKuen, Erikson & Stimson 1992, Stimson, MacKuen & Erikson 1995, Stimson 1999, Witko 2003, Wlezien 1995). Furthermore, the studies that do examine partisan groups find that Republicans, Independents, and Democrats have similar trends but different means, indicating the movement of opinion by partisan groups is essentially the same, but they have different starting points (Erikson, MacKuen & Stimson 2002, Gerber & Green 1999, Page & Shapiro 1992). The upshot of these analyses is that there are no differences in the opinion updating process for partisan groups.

The goal of this chapter is to show that updating by partisans does not follow parallel paths and the intensity of contemporary party polarization seems to make this all the more evident. Despite differences in micro and macro behavior, individual level studies of information processing (particularly those done in an experimental setting) can provide a foundation for an aggregate model of partisan information processing. Through their use of Taber and Lodge's theory of "motivated reasoning," Lebo and Cassino (2007) provide a useful first step towards bringing partisanship into our understanding of collective public opinion. Taber and Lodge (2006) argue that individual decision-making is connected to "consistency motivations" and these influence information processing and opinion updating. First, individuals tend to seek information that confirms prior beliefs. Second, when individuals do encounter conflicting information, they often discount or de-emphasize these messages. Furthermore, even when partisans hold the same factual beliefs, they tend to interpret these facts according to their partisan loyalties. For example, Democrats and Republicans who had similar estimates of the number of U.S. soldiers killed in Iraq disagreed on whether this number constituted a "large" or "small" number of casualties (Gaines et al. 2007). At least in experimental settings, partisanship influences what information individuals encounter, whether they accept or discount the information, and how they interpret it.

The importance of these findings for aggregate opinion is that we should not expect the public as a whole to operate like a neutral updater when linking information in the environment to collective public opinion. Segments of the public bring predispositions to the decision-making process and these should have important implications for the way that aggregate opinion evolves over time. As the previous chapter showed, the important "segments" for public opinion are partisan groups. As most studies of partisanship have shown, the fault lines for public opinion typically emerge over partisan control of the White House. Motivated reasoning extends the influence of partisanship to the aggregate level. When a Republican resides in the White House, Republicans will seek out information that things are going well or that the president is working effectively in order to maintain their existing beliefs and will tend to discount information that disconfirms their predispositions. At the same time, Democrats will seek out information that confirms their prior view that a Republican president is ineffective and should be held responsible for any adverse outcomes. What is important to recognize here is that in both cases the "priors" of partisans play an important role in how they update their opinions of things like presidential performance or economic outcomes.

Partisan Updating

There are two aspects of partisanship that influence aggregate behavior. In the first case, the role of partisanship is to shape the evaluations of party identifiers in their assessments of important political matters, like the performance of the president and the state of current economic conditions. The most straightforward description of this process is that Republicans will view the performance of Republican presidents more positively than Democrats and vice versa. However, as noted earlier, there is substantial evidence from experimental and individual-level studies that the process is somewhat more nuanced than this. The nuance arises from findings that individuals economize in their decision-making by relying on heuristics and shortcuts so that each time opinion is updated it is not based on a wholesale reassessment of relevant information, even by those with the highest levels of political sophistication. Instead, people develop a running tally that serve as priors when they update their opinions (Lodge & Taber 2013). Obviously, party cues are an essential part of this updating process, but drawing on the insights of these individual-level studies, the role of party cues are not the same for party supporters of presidents and their opponents. Supporters of the president will emphasize positive news about the president and economic conditions, activated by a confirmation bias. In other words, they tend to seek out information that confirms their preexisting, positive assessment of presidents from their party. Likewise, those from the out-party rely on motivated reasoning and look for information that will make it easier to support their prior assessment that a president from the opposite party will not perform well as president or as a steward of the economy.

Rating the Economy

Individual-level research suggests that the impact of partisanship on aggregate opinion emerges in both evaluative judgments, like the performance of the president, and more objective assessments, like the state of economic conditions (Gaines et al. 2007). Economic evaluations also offer a conservative test of partisan bias. Regular economic decisions, such as buying gas or groceries, create incentives for individuals to maintain accurate economic perceptions. Thus, if we find evidence of partisan differences on evaluations of the economy, it is likely that such differences would arise when examining other judgments like trust in government or the job performance of Congress.

An analysis of partisan economic evaluations requires construction of new measures in order to assess disaggregated economic evaluations by party. The standard measures of the public's views of the economy are derived from the Surveys of Consumers conducted by the University of Michigan. However, the Surveys of Consumers does not include questions about the respondents' partisan identification. So to assess the impact of partisanship on aggregate economic evaluations requires using other data sources, and in this analysis I use opinion data from Gallup, ABC, and CBS surveys. Since 1985, these survey organizations have regularly asked respondents about their evaluation of economic conditions.[1] In previous work with Peter Enns and Paul Kellstedt, we analyzed the *percentage* of the population giving a positive assessment of the economy (Enns, Kellstedt & McAvoy 2012, Enns & McAvoy 2012).[2] However, the calculation of the percentage giving a positive or negative approval works well at capturing partisan evaluations and differences when the economy is in "ordinary" times, but during the extraordinary times, like those seen since 2008, some of the partisan differences are hidden. For example, at the start of the Obama administration, the Gallup survey revealed similarly small percentages of Democrats and Republicans reporting that the economy was excellent or good, but there were important differences in how many in each party rated the economy as only fair or poor. To capture these differences, I recalculated the partisan evaluations for the Gallup, CBS, and ABC surveys using the average, rather than the percentage, yielding a measure that runs from 1 to 4. This makes it feasible to identify some of the subtle changes in assessment that can better capture partisan differences in respondents' evaluations of the economy.[3] I combine the three surveys into a single index of economic evaluations, with a one indicating that respondents felt that the economy was performing badly and a four indicating that it was performing well.[4] Because each of the surveys skipped some months, using data from all the surveys helps overcome the missing data problem that would occur if a single survey was relied upon. But equally important, combining surveys in the months where they overlap (a majority of time points), decreases the sampling error because the total sample size increases. Thus, we can disaggregate by partisanship and still obtain an accurate estimate of the subgroup's rating of the economy.

Figure 3.1 shows this series plotted by partisan group. A partisan pattern emerges with those from the president's party showing a more positive evaluation of the economy than Independents or those who identify with the opposition party. The pattern emerges more clearly in recent years, with Republicans viewing the economy much more positively during the administration of George W. Bush than Democrats or Independents, and Democrats reporting a better evaluation of the economy during the first term of President Obama than the other two groups. The only exception to this pattern is during the economic expansion that occurred during much of the Clinton administration. Despite anecdotal assessments of the Clinton administration as an intensely partisan period, evaluations of the economy by Democrats, Republicans, and Independents were remarkably similar, suggesting that steady reports of good economic news can help overcome partisan predispositions.

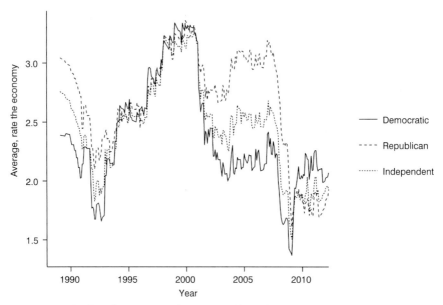

FIGURE 3.1   Rating the economy by party (1989 to 2012)

The changes in partisan evaluation of the economy at transition points are noteworthy. In Feb 2001, almost immediately after George Bush was sworn in as president, Democrats' evaluation of the economy fell from 3.2 to 2.8 and continued to decline for Bush's tenure in office. Consistent with the partisan divide that has characterized politics in the twenty-first century thus far, Republicans' view of the economy remained positive throughout most of George Bush's two terms in office, creating a wide gap between the parties in their view of economic conditions until the financial crisis of 2008. At the start of President Obama's presidency, Democrats rated economic conditions slightly worse than Republicans, but by April 2009, Republicans' evaluation of the economy fell as Democrats' assessment rose and the pattern of higher evaluations from the in-party and lower support from the out-party returned. Given the intensity of the partisan divide in recent years one is tempted to say that these differences are expected; however, we should pause and take note of the remarkable reach of partisanship that these differences imply. Not only do partisan evaluations color our assessment of the performance of the president but also our assessment of the performance of the economy.

These results provide important new information about the behavior of aggregate opinion. The effects of partisanship on public opinion generally are well documented, but its role in a more objective, over-time assessment of something like economic conditions is especially noteworthy. First, it suggests that partisans react quite differently to similar information about economic conditions, and importantly, the impact of partisanship is not limited to differences in the mean evaluation of partisan groups, but the trends for partisan groups can be profoundly different as well. Previously, scholars of aggregate opinion argued that partisanship was limited to "differences in means," but the analysis of economic evaluations presented here shows that, while this does occur, the more profound impact of partisanship, represented by differences in trends is common as well. This is especially evident in the highly partisan politics of the George W. Bush administration, where Democrats and Republicans came to markedly different conclusions about economic conditions. The significance of this finding extends into the operation of the economy as well, since frequently cited indexes of economic conditions like the Surveys of Consumers and the Confidence Boards Index of Leading Indicators rely in part on the public's assessment of economic conditions, and these indexes influence business leaders', political leaders', and consumers' decisions about spending and investment.[5]

Partisan Evaluations of Presidential Approval

Economic evaluations serve as a useful starting point for understanding the role of partisanship in aggregate public opinion, but to further advance this goal requires an assessment of presidential approval. For public opinion studies, the presidential approval series, pioneered by the Gallup organization, is unmatched in its frequency and duration. It, thus, provides a rich and unique context in which to explore the dynamics of public opinion and the role of partisanship, transitions and key events.

In Figure 3.2, presidential job approval is plotted on the same axis for Democrats and Republicans from the Kennedy to the Obama administration.[6] As the plot shows, there are clear changes at the start of each administration, with supporters of the incoming president increasing their support dramatically compared to their evaluation of the outgoing president. This increase among supporters averages 35.1 for both Democrats and Republicans. The increase in support for the new president by those from the outgoing party is much lower, 11.15. For Independents, approval of the president increases with a change in administration, but not to the level shown by the members of the president's party. Researchers examining these trends have at times made the case that there is little difference in the direction that partisans take in their evaluation of the president, it is merely the level of their support that is different—in other words, the means are different but the slopes are the same (Gerber & Green 1999, Erikson, MacKuen & Stimson 2002). Whatever the merits of this claim prior to 2001, the George W. Bush and Obama administrations certainly do not fit this pattern (see also, Jacobson 2006).[7] Democrats' support for the president fell sharply after 9/11, showed a modest increase at the start of the invasion

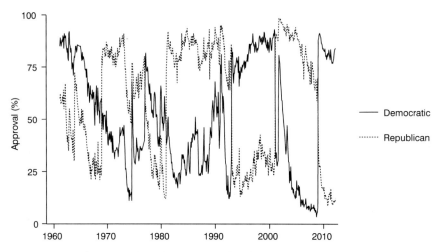

FIGURE 3.2 Gallup presidential job approval, Feb. 1961– Apr. 2012

of Iraq, but steadily declined thereafter, essentially bottoming out at 8 percent throughout 2007 and 2008. Republicans, on the other hand, were loyal to the president in their assessment of his job throughout 2005 and it wasn't until signs of fatigue regarding the war in Iraq and a weakening economy in 2007–2008 that a meaningful erosion of support for President Bush emerged. Through 2012, support for President Obama among Democrats held steady, while Republican support for the president fell almost immediately after his inauguration and remained very low throughout his first term. But the differences in trend between Democrats and Republicans during these two administrations clearly demonstrate that the dynamics of partisan presidential support are much more complex than a simple shift in the level of support depending on who occupies the White House.

The stark differences in the parties' evaluation of presidents from their party are further evident in a scatterplot of Democratic and Republican approval of the president (see Figure 3.3). The plot shows that Democrats and Republicans occupy different worlds when it comes to evaluation of the president and their evaluation is driven by which party controls the presidency. When a Democrat occupies the White House, Democratic approval is high and Republican approval is low, much lower than it ever gets when a Republican occupies the White House. Likewise, when a Republican is president, Republicans' approval moves to a much higher level, and Democratic approval moves to its lowest levels. When a Democrat is in office, approval ranges from 37 percent to 93 percent for Democrats and 8 percent to 72 percent for Republicans. When a Republican is president, Democratic approval ranges from 3 percent to 81 percent and Republican approval ranges from a low of 48 percent to a high of

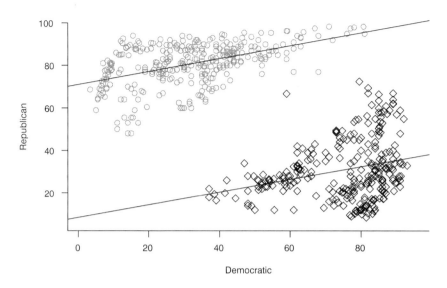

FIGURE 3.3 Gallup presidential job approval for Democrats and Republicans, Feb. 1961–Apr. 2012. Circles represent Republican administrations and diamonds are Democratic

98 percent. There is a tendency for partisans to put aside their partisanship and approve of the job a president from the opposite party, but partisans are loathe to voice weak support for a president from their own party.

Additional insight, and, in some ways a clearer picture, emerges by recasting the data as in-party and out-party assessments of presidential job approval and abandoning for the moment the idea of distinctly Democratic and Republican evaluations. This presentation of the data is reported in Figure 3.4. The average support for presidents by those loyal to them is 78 percent with a standard deviation of 11.7. The steady support for presidents by their followers is consistent with the argument for motivated reasoning. Partisans loyal to presidents are reluctant to abandon them, even when much of the news about them is bad. For example, just prior to Nixon's resignation in 1974 about 50 percent of Republicans still reported a positive assessment of his job approval (this is in contrast to the 11 percent approval rating by Democrats and 24 percent rating by Independents). As the figure shows, there are only three time periods when approval of presidents by their own party falls below 60 percent: Lyndon Johnson at the end of his second term, Nixon after Watergate and George W. Bush at the time of the 2008 financial crisis.

The evaluation of the president by those loyal to the opposition party reveals quite different dynamics. The out-party mean evaluation of the president's job approval is 31 percent and the standard deviation for this measure is 15.2. Thus, there is much more volatility in the views of those who oppose the president.

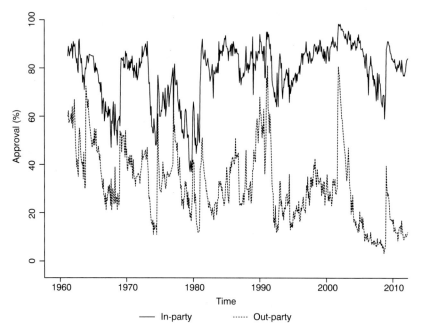

FIGURE 3.4 In-party vs. out-party, Gallup presidential job approval, Mar. 1961–Apr. 2012

This too is consistent with the motivated reasoning argument; those opposing presidents are generally looking for reasons to tie bad economic or political news to a president whom they do not support.[8] This effect is particularly pronounced in the Bush and Obama years, as the limited support each president had from the opposition quickly eroded after they took office. However, one distinctive feature of the series runs counter to this partisan opposition argument and it is the many upward spikes in this series as political events lead those from the opposition party to temporarily turn off their partisan filter and "rally" around the president. This too explains the higher volatility in the out-party series than the in-party series. For the in-party, there are no negative spikes that match the dramatic surges in approval of the president during times of national crisis.

Signal and Noise in Partisan Opinion

As was shown in the previous chapter, the signal-to-noise ratio helps identify when time series are moving in a consistent and clear direction and when movement is nothing more than noise around a weak signal. In the analysis of presidential approval and consumer sentiment, the analysis showed that aggregate public opinion is typically characterized by a strong signal and relatively minor noise. The signal-to-noise ratio can also help explain the characteristics

TABLE 3.1 Signal to noise ratio, in-party vs. out-party for presidential approval, 1961–2012

	σ_ω^2 *(Signal)*	σ_v^2 *(Noise)*	*Signal-to-noise ratio*
In-party	12.82	4.18	3.06
Out-party	29.34	2.78	10.77
Overall approval	20.7	0.36	59.14

of time series that are disaggregated by party. Given the importance of motivated reasoning in public opinion, the clear expectation is that those opposing the president are likely to respond more directly to changes in the political and economic environment and, thus, these series should show a higher signal-to-noise ratio. Although those loyal to the president are likely to be slower to respond to information, we would still expect some signal in their opinion, just not at the level exhibited by those looking for reasons to lower their opinion of a president.

As before, it is useful to look at the case of presidential approval, where sharp partisan effects are more clearly expected than in economic evaluations. A summary evaluation is possible by examining the series transformed into in-party and out-party approval. The results of this analysis are reported in Table 3.1. The differences between the in-party and out-party are quite dramatic, with a signal-to-noise ratio for supporters of the president of 3 to 1 (12.8 to 4.17) while the signal-to-noise ratio for the out-party is nearly 11 to 1. Thus, the approval of the president by the out-party has much more signal, than those identifying with the president's party. This finding squares with the partisan theory of motivated reasoning in which supporters of the president are reluctant to change their high opinion of the incumbent, so we observe some random fluctuations around a fairly consistent signal. On the other hand, those from the out-party readily update their views producing a sharp signal and very little noise.

Table 3.1 also includes the signal-to-noise ratio for overall approval. The signal-to-noise ratio is very high, indicating that nearly all of the updating is due to change in the observed series. In other words, if the updating is a weighted average of the variance of the signal and the measurement error, nearly all the weight is attributed to the signal. The strength of the signal is a byproduct of the strong signal that arises from transitions. As the Figures 3.2 and 3.4 show, the series show dramatic and rapid updating during presidential transitions. Whatever citizens perceived and imagined shortcomings, they do update along party lines as soon as a transition in the White House occurs. Elections focus citizens' attention on the executive and produce dramatic and plausible changes in public opinion.

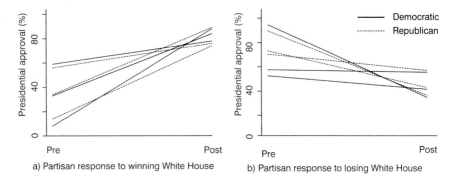

FIGURE 3.5 Immediate response to change of administration

Presidential Transitions

As the signal-to-noise analysis suggests, presidential transitions can help reveal the nature of the signal in aggregate time series like presidential approval. Looking again at Figure 3.2, it is clear that sharp differences arise at the time of partisan change in control of the White House. Given the variation in the strength of people's partisanship and in their attention to news, this change is striking. One could imagine a much more gradual transformation rather than the abrupt one that is observed, but partisan cues make this updating easy.

This effect is examined more fully in Figure 3.5 where the change before and after party control of the presidency is plotted. These before and after values are the immediate response to the change in administration as estimated from an autoregressive integrated moving average (ARIMA) intervention model.[9] We see that the change in approval for the winning party spikes dramatically upward in nearly all cases, while the losing party's support for the president falls (as expected), but not nearly as much as the winning party rises. Likewise, this spike for the in-party takes approximately two years to fully dissipate, whereas the change for the out-party dissipates in about a year. Thus, much of the increase in presidential approval at the time of a transition is due to the exuberance of those aligned with the winner. This has important implications for the dynamics of presidential approval past the point of the transition since, as we have seen, approval tends to remain high among the president's supporters.

Overall, this analysis shows that transitions are best characterized as moments when partisans differences are effectively "reset." This resetting means that partisans aligned with the new president will increase their average level of support and because of motivated reasoning, these exuberant partisans are likely to maintain their support even if economic conditions and political events might be expected to erode approval of the president. Brody (1991) and others argue that there is an inevitable downward trajectory from presidential approval as news stories about a newly elected president turn from favorable (give the president a chance) to more negative stories and opinions about the performance of new president are aired. But, the analysis presented here shows that the response of the in-party is much different than the out-party, and that much of the public (those from the president's party) are likely to be resistant to negative news for a long time.

Events

Researchers who study collective public opinion over time established long ago the importance of key events in the evolution of opinion (Mueller 1970, Gronke & Newman 2003, Newman & Forcehimes 2010). Important events like presidential assassinations, natural disasters, the start of international conflicts, and the terrorist attacks of 9/11 can fundamentally restructure public opinion at the moment that they occur as well as the trajectory of opinion in subsequent months and even years. Many such events are categorized as "rally events," signaling the way that the public comes together in moments of crisis.

Looking through the lens of partisanship, events are in many ways the opposite of transitions. Positive events mark an erosion of partisan differences. Since presidents tend to maintain high support within their party over time, the "rally around the flag" phenomenon is principally the byproduct of movement by the out-party toward the president. The terrorist attacks of 9/11 clearly illustrate this effect. In their approval of George W. Bush from September 4–5, 2001 to September 20–21, 2001, Democrats increased their approval by 57 percentage points. Republican support rose a much more modest 12 percentage points, but since it was already at 87 percent before the attack, it had much less room to rise. Clearly, the overwhelming movement in approval is due to the change in support by Democrats after the attack. Despite the "rally event," immediately after it, Democratic support began its downward spiral, while Republican approval hovered around 90 percent the remainder of George W. Bush's first term.[10]

Further analysis makes it possible to assess the duration of events like 9/11 and the start of the Gulf War on public opinion by calculating how long it takes for the spike that occurred at the start of these events to dissipate. For the 9/11 and the Gulf War (events that led to two of the highest values for presidential approval), 70 percent of the effect had disappeared in the first six months after these events occurred and nearly all of the effect was gone after a year. This is fairly similar to the duration of transitions in party control of the White House (i.e., Nixon, Carter, Clinton, G.W. Bush, Obama).

The Gulf War and 9/11 are not typical events, however, so it is worth examining the duration of some other key events like the capture of Manuel Noriega in January 1990, the start of the Iranian hostage crises in November 1979, and the assassination attempt on Ronald Reagan in April 1981. Although each of these events had a positive effect on presidential approval, the intervention analysis indicates that the impact of these was short-lived since presidential approval typically returned to the pre-event level after one month. Although these cases serve as examples, the analysis by Newman and Forcehimes (2010) of all events thought to influence presidential approval from 1953–2006 shows that most coded events have a limited impact on presidential approval in the short run (i.e., they are of short duration).

There are two lessons to take away from this examination of events and aggregate opinion. The first is that for major political events, partisans are able to put aside their natural loyalty to their party during times of crisis, and much of the movement that arises from these "rally events" is the result of the out-party moving from a low level of support for the incumbent president to an assessment much closer to the opinion of partisan supporters of the president. There is limited opportunity for those from the president's party to further signal their support because their support is already so high (i.e., there are ceiling effects). The second lesson is that many events are of relatively short duration, and this is due, in part, to the fact that partisans quickly return to their "typical" evaluation of the president after these events (Newman & Forcehimes 2010).

Policy Preferences

The issues considered thus far—perceptions of the economy and presidential performance—are both strongly influenced by economic concerns, and economic issues slot easily into existing partisan cues. In order to broaden the analysis, I examine survey questions that ask respondents about their policy preferences on issues that are not as closely linked to the economy. For this analysis, I turn to the General Social Survey (GSS) since this survey has asked respondents about their policy preferences on issues since 1973. The GSS assesses respondents' policy preferences by asking about current spending levels on a variety of social, health, and environmental issues. Respondents are asked if they think that spending on these issues is too little, about right, or too much. Answers to these spending questions are thought to reflect respondents' priorities or commitments to issues rather than their knowledge about existing budgetary matters. Scholars interested in policy preferences, particularly preferences over time, have turned to the GSS questions to measure them (Enns & Kellstedt 2008, Erikson, MacKuen & Stimson 2002, Stimson 2004).[11]

When looking at partisan support for issues over time, it is important to consider which party is traditionally stronger on a specific issue, or in other words, which party "owns" a particular issue. The idea of issue ownership developed in the context of the study of political campaigns and signified that one party was particularly trusted or strong on a specific issue. For example,

Republicans have generally been more trusted by the public on foreign policy issues and Democrats on social issues, such as social security. However, those studying public opinion over time have also seen periods of issue ownership, but the party that owns an issue can shift over time, either because of events or because of a deliberate strategy of persuasion and rhetoric by one party to control an issue (Holian 2004, Jacobs & Shapiro 2000).

With issue ownership and issue salience in mind, I focus the analysis of policy preferences on crime, the environment, and education from the GSS from 1973 to 2012. These issues are among the most salient ones on the political agenda, although the degree of salience does shift over time. More importantly, these issues vary in terms of issue ownership. The environment is an example of an issue dominated by one party throughout the years the GSS has collected this data. The Democrats have clearly owned this issue and when respondents indicate that they would like more spending on this issue, they are siding with the Democratic party. Thus, we would expect a high degree of partisan bias on this issue, with Democrats showing support for this issue more readily than Republicans. In addition, it is likely that the partisan bias would grow over time in concert with the increased polarization in recent years. The other issues, crime and education, have more complex histories in terms of issue ownership. The public generally favors the "tough on crime" position, the position traditionally associated with the Republican party. However, as Holian (2004) shows, President Clinton was able to "steal" this issue from Republicans in the 1990s by staking out a more centrist (or some Democrats would say conservative) position and captured the support of those citizens endorsing the tough on crime position. On the other hand, public education has traditionally been a Democratic issue, but Republicans, under George W. Bush, fought hard to win public support for his "No Child Left Behind" policies. Thus, these issues allow us to look at partisan differences in preferences on an issue owned by one party as well as two issues in which the parties contested for control.

Because the GSS provides three choices to respondents on these spending questions (spending is too little, about right, or too much), Tom W. Smith, one of the leading analysts of GSS data, recommends creating a net support variable. To do this, the percent indicating that there is too much funding for an issue is subtracted from the percent saying that there is too little. Positive numbers indicate the public prefers more spending in that area; negative numbers mean the public thinks that there should be less spending for that issue. This results in a measure for support that can range from 100 (everyone thinks that there is too little funding) to –100 (everyone thinks that there is too much funding). Therefore, years with positive numbers indicate that the public as a whole thinks that there is not enough funding. As Smith notes, the public generally supports more spending on the issues asked in the GSS, even though they support less spending overall (Smith 2013).

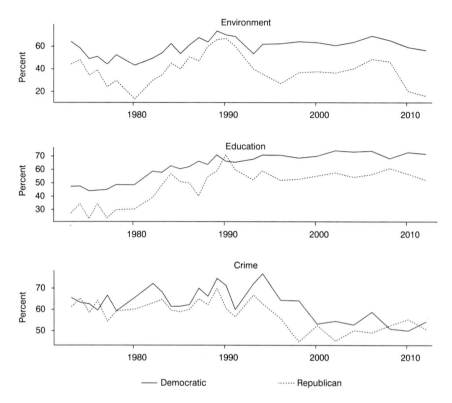

FIGURE 3.6 Spending preferences from the General Social Survey for the environment, education, and crime by party (1973–2012)

The responses to the three spending questions are reported in Figure 3.6 each broken down by party. For these questions, those identified in the survey as Independents were allocated to the party that they lean towards. The first panel in Figure 3.6 shows the results for Democrats' and Republicans' preference of more spending on the environment. As expected, Democrats favored spending over this time period more than Republicans. What is interesting, however, is the sharp divergence that arises in the mid-1990s, indicating real party differences into the 2010s. Perhaps even more remarkable is the chasm that emerges between the two parties beginning in 2010. Republicans dropped nearly all their support for spending on the environment in the wake of the recession beginning late in 2008. (This effect is not fully captured in the survey until 2010 since that was the first survey conducted after the recession.) The wide gap persisted in the 2012 survey. The lesson here is clearly that issue ownership leads to sharp partisan divisions.

The second and third panels in Figure 3.6 show the support for more spending on crime and education by partisan group. Support for more spending on education bears some similarities to the party differences that emerged on the environment, with a gap developing in the 1990s. In this case, however, the gap doesn't continue to grow throughout the 2000s but stays relatively constant. Simply looking at the trends of each party reveals an interesting pattern: Democrats show a steady rise in support for more spending on education, while Republican support shows more volatility.[12]

The plot of preferences for crime shows little in the way of partisan differences. Both Democrats and Republicans fluctuate in their preference for more spending to reduce crime. Democrats' preferences for spending on crime fluctuates a lot from the 1970s to the mid-1990s, but somewhat surprisingly, Republicans tend to match these fluctuations for the most part. Both parties seemed to endorse Clinton's push for more spending in the mid-1990s. After the mid-1990s, there is a near consensus among Democrats and Republicans that more spending on crime is not as urgent as it was in the 1970s and 1980s.

Overall, this analysis of policy preferences reveals that partisan differences play an important role in the dynamics of aggregate opinion. Only on the issue of crime were the trends for Democrats and Republicans aligned. For preferences about the environment and education, support for spending was markedly different with Republicans generally wanting a smaller increase than Democrats. It is important to recognize that the trends on these issues for the party groups generally seem to fluctuate in response to real events in the political environment. Party differences regarding the environment can reasonably be thought of as different priorities for the parties. In the wake of the 2008 recession, Republicans by and large felt that environmental concerns were less of a concern than before the recession, while Democrats maintained steady support. Thus, even on issues of spending priorities, the public's response is not random noise, but is instead, influenced by events but structured by partisan concerns.

Summary

Building on the signal and noise theme, this chapter accounts further for the nature of the signal in aggregate opinion. Much of the signal is the byproduct of partisan updating associated with predictable changes in the environment like elections and surprise events. The analysis shows that events like presidential transitions and rally events change the dynamics of public opinion, effectively resetting partisan evaluations. This is one of the clearest cases of "partisan polarization," if polarization is defined as partisans moving in opposite direction in terms of their opinion (Bullock 2009). This suggests that rather than having fixed priors, partisans reset their priors, particularly at times of presidential transitions. In general, supporters of the new president move in a sharply positive direction at the time of a transition, and those supporting the opposing party move downward, although not to the same degree. But as noted, the change is not just captured by mean difference, but the speed of change and trend vary for supporters of the two major parties. Looking at the in-party versus out-party analysis shows us that priors matter more for the in-party than the out-party. Thus, one of the key findings is a confirmation of the idea that motivated reasoning takes on a different character for those supporting presidents than those opposing them.

Similar patterns emerge for party groups when examining questions about the public's evaluation of the economy as for presidential approval. This similarity helps demonstrate the power of partisan thinking since the questions that the public are asked to evaluate, job approval of the president and current economic conditions, are quite different in terms of what respondents are required to assess.

Putting party at the center of collective rationality upends the typical explanation for why aggregate opinion is coherent and stable. If party provides the structure or signal for aggregate opinion, then it is harder to subscribe to the "miracle of aggregation" argument and the idea that whatever misjudgments are made by the uninformed are balanced out by the attentive public, who can be counted on to provide a clear indication about the public's attitudes and intentions. The centrality of parties to the political process is not new, however. The responsible party argument developed in the 1950s endorses the idea that strong parties are a necessary feature of modern democracies, structuring politics both inside and outside of government.

The analysis thus far examines the dynamics of aggregate opinion by looking primarily at trends, deviations from trend (i.e., random errors) and transition points but has not investigated the use of key information. The next step is to assess more fully the use of information in updating, particularly in partisan updating. The following chapter outlines a model of Bayesian updating that incorporates a role for priors as a mechanism for weighing new information relevant to the updating process. This marks an important departure from the standard approach to updating opinion which assumes that all available information is incorporated into changes in opinion.

Appendix: Signal to Noise Ratios by Presidential Administration

Table 3.2 shows the signal-to-noise ratio for presidential approval for each of the presidents from Kennedy to Obama. As anticipated, the overall pattern is that the aggregate opinion for those opposed to the incumbent president contains more signal than the opinion of a president's supporters. This holds true for Kennedy, Reagan, George H.W. Bush, and George W. Bush. For president Obama, support among Democrats does not vary much, but the noise

TABLE 3.2 Signal-to noise-ratio, presidential approval, 1961–2012

President	Democrat			Republican		
	σ_ω^2 (Signal)	σ_v^2 (Noise)	Signal-to-noise ratio	σ_ω^2 (Signal)	σ_v^2 (Noise)	Signal-to-noise ratio
Kennedy	6.77	4.98	1.36	69.71	7.43	9.38
Johnson	4.51	8.72	0.52	6.54	8.41	0.77
Nixon	8.31	4.26	1.95	17.83	1.28	13.95
Ford	14.07	10.10	1.39	11.45	7.57	1.51
Carter	29.16	0.30	97.20	25.11	3.60	6.97
Reagan	19.14	0.01	All signal★	5.01	5.27	0.95
G.H.W. Bush	63.24	1.40	45.06	19.86	5.97	3.33
Clinton	3.15	4.01	0.79	5.90	7.73	0.76
G.W. Bush	24.8	0.01	All signal★	4.26	3.84	1.11
Obama	2.52	0.09	25.20	6.36	0.00	All signal★

★Noise component so small that the series is nearly all signal.

component is fairly small, leading to a relatively high signal-to-noise ratio (but not as high as for Republicans during his administration). As the table shows, there are some exceptions to this overall pattern. The movement of partisan approval for Johnson and Clinton was not especially consistent, leading to a low signal-to-noise ratio for both presidents. Approval for Nixon and Carter was more varied for their supporters than for their opposition, primarily because both had notable changes in support towards the end of their administrations (although Nixon was in the end more popular with Republicans than Carter was with Democrats).

Notes

1. The Gallup question asks, "How would you rate economic conditions in this country today—as excellent, good, only fair, or poor?" CBS asks, "How would you rate the condition of the national economy these days? Is it very good, fairly good, fairly bad, or very bad?" The ABC surveys ask, "Do you think the nation's economy is getting better, worse, or staying about the same?" In the questions used to identify partisanship, respondents were asked whether "you usually consider yourself a Republican, Democrat or Independent."

2. For the Gallup series, the percent rating the economy as excellent or good was tabulated, and for the CBS series, the percent rating the economy as very good or fairly good was calculated. For ABC, the percent saying the economy was getting better is tabulated.

3. Because all three survey organizations ordered their questions with low scores as a positive evaluation, I reversed the ordering of the measure so that high scores are associated with a positive evaluation. Researchers typically want to know whether good economic conditions correspond to positive economic evaluations and this change makes that feasible.

4. I combine the series using a technique for merging time series described in Shumway and Stoffer (2006). This procedure is similar to Stimson's (1999) dyad ratios algorithm but Stimson's procedure is built to handle survey percentages, rather than the mean score evaluation used here. Both algorithm scales the series to a common metric and then use a factor analytic approach to extract the common variance of the series.

5. See Enns and McAvoy (2012) and Enns, Kellstedt, and McAvoy (2012) for more detailed analyses of economic conditions and partisan evaluations.

6. Independents are consistently in between supporters of the two major parties.

7. A more detailed graph of the Bush and Obama years is available in the online supplement at http://gemcavoy.wp.uncg.edu/cpr/.

8. This disparity in volatility is graphically represented in figure in the online supplement at http://gemcavoy.wp.uncg.edu/cpr/.

9. In the language of ARIMA modeling, a zero-order transfer function means that the effect of an event or transitions between administrations will be immediate and short-lived. It is possible that political events might follow a zero-order transfer function, but the impact of transitions between administrations should be an immediate change, followed by a gradual decline. This is most appropriately modeled as a first-order transfer function with a pulse function (McCleary & Hay, Jr. 1980). This analysis relies on code originally written by Jamie Monogan (http://spia.uga.edu/faculty_pages/monogan/teaching/ts/, accessed February 8, 2015).

10. A graph of the partisan differences is available in the online supplement at http://gemcavoy.wp.uncg.edu/cpr/.
11. Despite the general high quality of the GSS, its major liability is its irregular administration. It began as an annual survey but skipped the years 1979, 1981, 1992, 1995, and 1997. Since 1998, it has been conducted biennially.
12. There is a slight rise in support in 2002 associated with the "No Child Left Behind" policies of George W. Bush, but other fluctuations in support need further examination.

Bibliography

Bartels, Larry. 2002. "Beyond the Running Tally: Partisan Bias in Political Perceptions." *Political Behavior* 24(2):117–150.

Brody, Richard A. 1991. *Assessing the President: The Media, Elite Opinion, and Public Support.* Stanford, CA: Stanford University Press.

Bullock, John G. 2009. "Partisan Bias and the Bayesian Ideal in the Study of Public Opinion." *Journal of Politics* 71(3):1109–1124.

De Boef, Suzanna & Paul M. Kellstedt. 2004. "The Political (and Economic) Origins of Consumer Confidence." *American Journal of Political Science* 48(4):633–649.

Enns, Peter. K. & Gregory E. McAvoy. 2012. "The Role of Partisanship in Aggregate Opinion." *Political Behavior* 34(4):627–651.

Enns, Peter K. & Paul M. Kellstedt. 2008. "Policy Mood And Political Sophistication: Why Everybody Moves Mood." *British Journal of Political Science* 38(Part 3):433–454.

Enns, Peter K., Paul M. Kellstedt & Gregory E. McAvoy. 2012. "The Consequences of Partisanship in Economic Perceptions." *Public Opinion Quarterly* 76(2):287–310.

Erikson, Robert S., Michael B. MacKuen & James A. Stimson. 2002. *The Macro Polity.* New York: Cambridge University Press.

Gaines, Brian J., James H. Kuklinski, Paul J. Quirk, Buddy Peyton & Jay Verkuilen. 2007. "Same Facts, Different Interpretations: Partisan Motivation and Opinion on Iraq." *Journal of Politics* 69(4):957–974.

Gerber, Alan & Donald Green. 1999. "Misperceptions about Perceptual Bias." *Annual Review of Political Science* 2(1):189–210.

Gronke, Paul & Brian Newman. 2003. "FDR to Clinton, Mueller to?: A Field Essay on Presidential Approval." *Political Research Quarterly* 56:501–512.

Holian, David B. 2004. "He's Stealing My Issues! Clinton's Crime Rhetoric and the Dynamics of Issue Ownership." *Political Behavior* 26(2):95–124.

Jacobs, Lawrence R. & Robert Y. Shapiro. 2000. *Politicians Don't Pander: Political Manipulation and the Loss of Democratic Responsiveness.* Chicago, IL: University of Chicago Press.

Jacobson, Gary C. 2006. *Divider, Not a Uniter: George W. Bush and the American People.* New York: Pearson Longman.

Lebo, Matthew. J. & Daniel. Cassino. 2007. "The Aggregated Consequences of Motivated Reasoning and the Dynamics of Partisan Presidential Approval." *Political Psychology* 28(6):719–746.

Lodge, Milton. & Charles S. Taber. 2013. *The Rationalizing Voter.* Cambridge: Cambridge University Press.

MacKuen, Michael B., Robert S. Erikson & James A. Stimson. 1992. "Peasants or Bankers: The American Electorate and the U.S. Economy." *American Political Science Review* 86(3):597–611.

McCleary, Richard. & Richard A. Hay, Jr. 1980. *Applied Time Series Analysis*. Beverly Hills, CA: Sage.

Mueller, John. 1970. "Presidential Popularity from Truman to Johnson." *American Political Science Review* 65:18–34.

Newman, Brian & Andrew Forcehimes. 2010. "Rally Round the Flag Events for Presidential Approval Research." *Electoral Studies* 29(1):144–154.

Page, Benjamin I. & Robert Y. Shapiro. 1992. *The Rational Public: Fifty Years of Trends in Americans' Policy Preferences*. Chicago, IL: University of Chicago Press.

Shumway, Robert H. & David S. Stoffer. 2006. *Time Series Analysis and Its Applications: With R Examples*. New York: Springer.

Smith, Tom W. 2013. *Trends in National Spending Priorities 1973–2012*. Technical report. Chicago, IL: National Opinion Research Center

Stimson, James A. 1999. *Public Opinion in America: Moods, Cycles, and Swings*. 2nd edition. Boulder, CO: Westview Press.

Stimson, James A. 2004. *Tides of Consent: How Public Opinion Shapes American Politics*. New York and London: Cambridge University Press.

Stimson, James A., Michael B. MacKuen & Robert S. Erikson. 1995. "Dynamic Representation." *American Political Science Review* 89(3):543–565.

Stokes, Donald E. 1966. "Some Dynamic Elements of Contests for the Presidency." *The American Political Science Review* 60(1):19–28.

Taber, Charles S. & Milton Lodge. 2006. "Motivated Skepticism in the Evaluation of Political Beliefs." *American Journal of Political Science* 50(3):755–769.

Witko, Christopher. 2003. "Cold War Belligerence and U.S. Public Opinion Toward Defense Spending." *American Politics Research* 31(4):379–403.

Wlezien, Christopher. 1995. "The Public as Thermostat: Dynamics of Preferences for Spending." *American Journal of Political Science* 39(4):981–1000.

4

INFORMATION PROCESSING AND SELECTIVE ATTENTION

Given the range of issues and the wealth of information that constitute the modern political environment, it is not surprising that citizens require partisanship to help structure public opinion. The characterization of the ideal citizen as someone who contemplates current events and rationally chooses among alternatives is overly optimistic, at best, or naive, at worst. Instead, citizens, even the best-informed, lean heavily on party cues to formulate decisions (Gaines et al. 2007, Taber & Lodge 2006). Rather than neutral information processors, citizens interpret facts to fit their existing view points and those who are more informed tend to be better at incorporating new information into their partisan interpretation of political affairs (Gaines et al. 2007). With new and complex issues making their way to the top of the political agenda, it is not surprising that citizens, even well-intentioned ones, rely on party cues to sift through the wealth of information. Again, this leads citizens to rely on motivated reasoning, that is, they seek out information that is consistent with their preconceptions (or priors) and ignore, discount, or counter-argue information that is inconsistent with their predispositions.

In addition to partisan concerns, citizens' use of information to update their opinions is influenced by the complexity of political decision-making (i.e., a wide range of shifting issues) and by their limited attention to politics (by choice or necessity). Thus, a model of *political* information processing at the aggregate level must incorporate two deviations from strict rationality: partisanship and limited use of available information. In this chapter, I describe a model of information processing of aggregate opinion that highlights both partisanship and shifting attention. The Bayesian updating process that serves as a foundation for the information processing model emphasizes "strong" and "weak" priors and facilitates the incorporation of political exigencies, like partisanship and shifting attention.

Information Processing

The previous chapters emphasized the importance of partisanship to aggregate public opinion and outlined the motivated reasoning argument and its implications for the updating process. But, it is important to note that despite its overriding importance to the evolution of public opinion, there are other factors to incorporate into an updating model. For example, in his generative study of individual-level opinion, Zaller (1992) proposes a model of information processing that emphasizes information reception as a key component of the process by which individuals update in response to new information in the environment. Individuals' willingness to receive new information is contingent on their awareness and predispositions. Zaller and others recognize that individual citizens are occupied with a variety of tasks, such as family and work, and these preclude them from giving their full attention to events in the political and economic environment. Because of this shifting attention to politics, we would expect a certain amount of randomness in aggregate public opinion as the idiosyncrasies of daily life bring events into focus for some people while diverting it from others. As Zaller argues, a component of public opinion is the result of top-of-the-head evaluations in which people's responses are influenced by salient information and this adds some randomness to aggregate opinion.

Incorporating "priors" into a model of political updating is a marked contrast to conventional notions of aggregate updating and requires describing a different kind of model of political information processing. Outlining the Bayesian updating model and its application to economic evaluations and presidential approval requires a number of steps, so I provide the reader with a road map. The development of the model proceeds in three steps. I first lay the foundation for the Bayesian updating model with a brief description of Bayes' theorem. Next, to illustrate the role of priors in updating, I use an example of a change in opinion at one point in time and then extend this to look at opinion updating over time. The first two steps are necessary to understand the updating process. In the third step, I formally incorporate the role of information into the updating process. With the model defined, I illustrate the role of "priors" in evaluations of the economy, extend the analysis of priors to "partisan" information processing, and finally examine the variation in the public's attention and receptivity to economic information over time.

Bayes' Theorem as a Model of Collective Political Updating

In recent years, social scientists have leveraged the power of Bayesian analysis to shed insight on a number of important questions (for overviews, see Gelman et al. [2013], Jackman [2009], and Gill [2007]). At the heart of Bayesian analysis is the theorem of probability first proposed by Thomas Bayes in the eighteenth century.[1] My purpose in describing the logic of Bayes' theorem is to show how it serves as a foundation for thinking about collective information processing and opinion change.[2] As Bullock (2009, 1111) notes, within political science the debate about how Bayesian logic should be applied and what counts as evidence for Bayesian updating is ongoing, but:

> Bayesian models of public opinion can be heuristically useful even if we wrongly assume that people are Bayesians, because they offer a systematic way to account for the relative influences of old beliefs and new information.

At its core, Bayes' theorem describes a process in which prior beliefs are updated in response to new information to provide an updated opinion, described as the posterior belief (Jackman 2009, xxvii). This type of reasoning seems very intuitive, particularly when thinking about public opinion (but also in a host of other settings).[3] When making decisions in light of new information, individuals do not revise their opinions anew—they draw upon past opinions and weigh new information through the lens of prior beliefs. So, for example, if people are asked about their confidence in the US education system in light of news reports about American students' performance relative to students in other countries, they are likely to assess that information contingent upon their prior beliefs about American education. Those who are confident in their prior assessment of the education system are not likely to move dramatically in their judgment based on one new piece of information (i.e., they have strong priors, a high degree of certainty). On the other hand, people who are uncertain about the current performance of the education system are likely to be heavily influenced by new information (i.e., they have weak priors and thus are more influenced by the data). The ways in which people update in a manner consistent with Bayes' theorem can be expressed more formally with reference to the theorem itself.

$$P(\theta|y) \propto P(y|\theta)P(\theta)$$

If θ represents the underlying parameter of interest—a respondent's evaluation of the education system—and y represents information about the education system, then the respondent's judgment in light of new information is $P(\theta|y)$, which is described as the posterior distribution of θ. The posterior is derived from the prior evaluation of the education system, $P(\theta)$, and the likelihood $P(y|\theta)$. The likelihood, $P(y|\theta)$, is the probability of the new report having the value y, given the results of prior evaluation, θ. If the US system had a good evaluation in the past, what is the probability of it having a good evaluation now, i.e., y is high.

Continuing with the issue of education policy, the top panel of Figure 4.1 characterizes the updating behavior of a person with a relatively pessimistic view

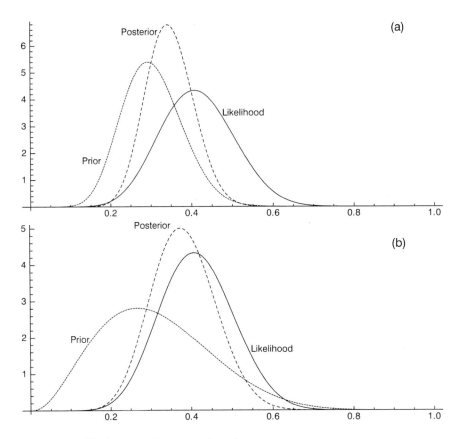

FIGURE 4.1 The impact of strong and weak priors

of the American education system, giving it a rating of 0.3 on a scale from 0 to 1, and with strong convictions, represented by a relatively narrow standard deviation of 0.073. The lower panel, represents the case of a person who is equally pessimistic, with the same 0.3 rating of the system, but has much less conviction as characterized by the wide distribution around the 0.3 rating (in this case the standard deviation is 0.14, nearly twice as wide as in the first case). If the results from a Trends in International Mathematics and Science Study (TIMSS) show American students improving their overall ranking, the first respondent is not likely to dramatically change their response in light of new information. As shown in the upper panel, the posterior (the updated evaluation by the respondent) remains relatively close to the prior. The second respondent with less certainty about their rating (a weaker prior) is more influenced by the news and their new rating (posterior) improves to 0.38.[4] Together Figures 4.1(a) and 4.1(b) demonstrate how the inclusion of priors into decision-making can alter how information gets used. In the first case, prior beliefs were stronger so while new information led opinion to change, it did not change very dramatically. In the second case, the impact of the new information was more pronounced because prior opinion was weaker or less certain.

Although this describes the typical decision-making process, there are situations in which the information itself is so overwhelming (or in the language of Bayesian analysis, so precise) that people will update their opinion no matter what their priors. As Petris and Petrone (2009, 27) say, "The more precise the observation is, or the more vague our initial information was, the more we 'trust the data'." This is why we have such dramatic reversals in support for presidents when historic events occur. Events like the Oklahoma bombing and 9/11 clearly convey a crisis situation and are nearly universally known. In the language of Bayesian analysis, this means that there is little uncertainty or variance in people's understanding of the importance of this information for updating opinions, and that prior information plays very little role in current updating.[5]

The discussion above shows how Bayes' theorem can describe a model of decision-making conditional on available information in the static case. However, an analysis of collective political rationality requires looking over time to understand the way that opinion is updated in light of the flow of information. The logic of Bayesian updating is similar to the static case since both situations assume that current decision-making is influenced by past choices as well as new information and the weight of new information can vary from strong to weak depending on the strength of the information and the strength of the prior. This kind of reasoning is easily integrated into the Kalman filter, a well-established approach to modeling data as they evolve over time (Gerber & Green 1998, Green, Palmquist & Schickler 2002).

Returning to the case in which respondents are asked to evaluate the US education system, let Y represent the opinion offered by a respondent in a survey and θ represent prior evaluations of the education system.

We can specify a model to connect a new observation and opinion over time as,

$$Y_t = \theta_t + \varepsilon_t$$

In addition, the path of the prior evaluation can be described as,

$$\theta_t = \theta_{t-1} + v_t$$

In this case, v_t is the error in updating that occurs as we move across time, and the variance of $v_t \left(\sigma_v^2 \right)$ represents the uncertainty associated with the prior, i.e., whether it is weak or strong. When the error variance in the prior is small, θ_t is known with some precision or certainty and when it is large, there is uncertainty about the value of θ_t. The uncertainty in the new opinion can be characterized by σ_ε^2, the variance of the noise in new observations. These variances are known as "conditional variances" because they are estimated based on information in previous observations.

Updating in light of new observations in the next time period leads to

$$\theta_1 = \theta_0 + K_1 \left(Y_1 - \theta_0 \right)$$

The "error" in updating is the difference between observed and prior opinion $(Y_1 - \theta_0)$ and it is the means by which "new" or "surprise" information enters the updating process. If the errors are large, this is a signal that opinion should be updated. If the errors are small, opinion should remain more or less the same. However, the movement associated with the error is weighted by K_1 where K_1 is the ratio of the error variance in the signal (σ_v^2) to the total variance $(\sigma_v^2 + \sigma_\varepsilon^2)$, variance in the signal plus the noise component. This represents the Kalman gain and it ranges from 0 to 1.

$$K_1 = \frac{\sigma_v^2}{\sigma_v^2 + \sigma_\varepsilon^2}$$

Thus, the weight of this ratio (i.e., the Kalman gain) is determined by the precision of the information. When σ_ε^2 is large relative to the prior error variance (indicating lots of random fluctuations in new opinions about the education system and thus uncertainty), the Kalman gain will approach zero and there will be little updating in light of new information. When the noise in the new observations is small relative to the variance in prior evaluations of the education system, the Kalman gain will be near one and there will be substantial updating in light of new observations. Consistent with Bayesian analysis, the data carry weight when they have a strong signal (Kalman gain approaches 1) and the prior dominates (little updating occurs) when there is uncertainty about the precision of the new observations.

The 2008 Republican primary helps to illustrate the role that priors can play in the way that aggregate opinion is updated. Although Governor Mitt Romney held an early advantage and eventually won the nomination, the middle stage of the primary reflected the uncertainty about who should represent the party in the general election. Thus, the fluidity of the support for the major candidates is a byproduct of the relatively weak priors of the party as a whole. It wasn't just that there was disagreement among Republican primary voters about whether to support a "fighter" like Newt Gingrich, a social conservative like Rick Santorum, or an established candidate like Mitt Romney, but that the support for each of them shifted over time. Figure 4.2 shows the support for some of the key Republican candidates as reported in Gallup tracking poll surveys of Republican voters. The figure shows the support for Romney, Gingrich, and Santorum, and the volatility of the tracking polls reflects the uncertainty among the party as a whole regarding who should be its nominee. The bottom of the figure tracks support for Ron Paul in the primaries. The steadiness of support for Paul stands in stark contrast to

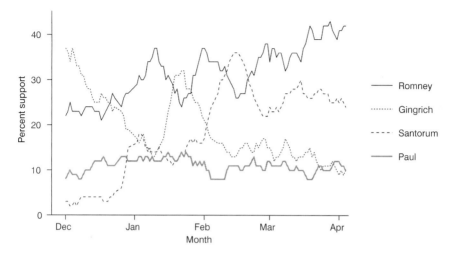

FIGURE 4.2   Tracking poll for Republican primary, 2012. Source: Gallup Poll

the fluidity of the other candidates. Whereas the support for the other candidates suggests weak priors and frequent updating in light of news from the campaign, Paul's loyal followers showed steadfast support for him and few outside of this loyal following joined in to support him. Thus, for the most part, it didn't matter whether the news about his campaign was good or bad his support was consistent.

The role of priors in the updating opinion about Mitt Romney by Republican party identifiers can be illustrated using the Kalman filter and its updating equations. To begin, a prior must be specified for the initial state of support for Governor Romney, θ_0 and initial system variance, σ_0^2, At the beginning of the primary season, we start the updating model by assuming that party identifiers as a whole did not have strong support for Romney and can be characterized as having a prior in the middle range of 50 and with a variance of 25 (or a standard deviation of 5), reflecting their uncertainty.[6] With these initial conditions, we can model the recursive decision-making of an individual.

If we begin with a prior of $\theta_0=50$, $K_1=.50$, and initial observation from a tracking poll indicates $Y_1=45$, we can update the evaluation of Republican voters of Romney as

$$\theta_1 = \theta_0 + K_1\left(Y_1 - \theta_0\right)$$
$$\theta_1 = 50 + 0.50 \times (45 - 50) = 47.5$$

In this case, the deviation between the prior and the observed value is –5, and since the Kalman gain is 0.50, half of this deviation is used to update the posterior so that the mean of its distribution is 47.5. (In addition, the uncertainty of the posterior is updated as well, but the calculation for updating the uncertainty of the posterior is rather involved and described in the appendix.) In this case, the uncertainty about θ_2 is approximately 11. Updating proceeds in an iterative fashion so that the posterior at t_1 becomes the prior at t_2. However, because the updating includes K, the Kalman gain, the weight of the prior in the updating procedure is influenced by it. When K is near 1 any difference between the prior and the observed value is treated as important and the full weight of this deviation is used to adjust the next observation. When K is small, any difference between the prior and the current observation is discounted, reducing the impact of any differences between what occurred and what was expected.

If the second assessment of Romney is very close to the first with $Y_2 = 44$, the posterior moves toward the observed value, with the posterior at t_2 equal to 46.07. This updating process continues over time as the posterior is estimated and becomes the prior for the Bayesian updating in the next time period.

Thus, the Kalman filter and its associated updating equations provide a framework for understanding Bayesian updating. At each point in time, the updating process relies on the past, in particular the best estimate of underlying opinion in the previous time period. How opinion evolves over time depends on the difference between what was expected (the prior) and what was observed (the latest poll results), and a weight (the Kalman gain) that helps determine how much updating should occur. Again, at times, opinion will change dramatically because the significance of "news" like an international crisis suggests a sharp departure from past behavior. But, barring such extraordinary conditions, opinion will be influence by recent experiences. If polling is done in the midst of uncertainty, a lot of change (or updating) will occur. If polling is conducted during a period of relative stability, change is likely to be small. Therefore, updating occurs through some mix of prior experience and general uncertainty about the current state of affairs.

It is important to note that the updating process described thus far does not actually measure information in the environment. The updating process proceeds as the result of measured opinion (not the "true" level of opinion) and its deviation from expectations. But, actual news and information, like current economic conditions, are not factored into this relatively sparse description of opinion evolution. However, in the next sections, the nature of information will be incorporated. The use of information in the updating process mirrors the process described here, since priors and their level of uncertainty drive the updating process.

In recent years, political scientists have debated the extent to which individuals and the public as a whole engage in Bayesian updating and its appropriateness as a description of the dynamics of opinion. At its heart, Bayesian updating is intended to provide a way to learn and improve decision-making in light of new information. In other words, those using Bayesian updating should make a more accurate assessment of conditions and more effectively use available information. According to Bullock (2009), to engage in

Bayesian updating, the public needs to appropriately weigh new information, but studies of political behavior suggest that partisanship leads individuals to "overweight" prior information, that is, they are not as responsive to new information as they should be. In addition, Kim, Taber, and Lodge (2010) argue that Bayesian updating cannot accommodate some of the features of political decision-making like persistence (lack of updating) and motivated reasoning (over- and under-reaction to political news) and that Bayesians must maintain "independence between priors and new evidence" (Taber & Lodge 2006, 767). However, despite these discrepancies between ideal Bayesian updating and what occurs in the world of public opinion, Bullock (2009) argues Bayesian analysis is useful because it approaches the study of public opinion from an information processing perspective, studying how the public adapts or learns in response to new information by updating its opinion. In addition to its focus on information processing, the tools for conducting Bayesian analysis over time make it feasible to identify deviations from an idealized Bayesian updating process (e.g., when a strong prior limits the weight of new information) and enhance our understanding of the underlying dynamics of aggregate opinion.

Model of Information Processing and Partisan Updating

The logic of the Bayesian updating process in the previous section can be extended to a model that includes explanatory factors. Now, opinion, Y_t, is the byproduct of its previous history, x_t, and exogenous changes, in this case changes in unemployment.

$$y_t = x_t + \beta_{1t} Unem_{t-1} + v_t$$
$$x_t = x_{t-1} + \omega_{1t}$$
$$\beta_{1t} = \beta_{1t-1} + \omega_{2t}$$

If we treat β as the weight assigned to observed information, using unemployment in this case, we want to know how this weight is updated over time in order to understand how information is being processed. The updating equation is:

$$\beta_t = \beta_{t-1} + K_t \eta_{t|t-1}$$

Thus, the current value of β_t is described as a weighted average of $\beta_t|\beta_{t-1}$ and the additional information that is carried in the prediction error, $\eta_{t|t-1}$. The gain, K_t, is the weight that is assigned to new information. In the Bayesian updating model, a change in opinion, as captured by the prediction error, is weighed by K_t, the Kalman gain. The Kalman gain is a way to keep track of whether opinion is stable or fluctuating. In other words, when there is some certainty about the model, a large prediction error is viewed as an anomaly and does not lead the public to rethink its current approach. As Wells (1996, 82) describes it:

> The more uncertain the state [underlying opinion], the greater the weight of the current observation in the revised or updated estimate of the state [underlying opinion]. Conversely, the more uncertain the observation is, the smaller is the weight applied to the current observation.

For the purposes of political information processing, all that remains is to show how political considerations might influence the updating process. If, because of partisan predispositions, supporters of the incumbent president are reluctant to view a president from their party unfavorably, they will be slow to update in light of unfavorable information. This will be reflected in the Kalman filter in two ways. First, the conditional variance will be small, consistent with a strong prior, (i.e, strong beliefs that "their" president is performing well). Second, the Kalman gain will be smaller (closer to zero), meaning that new information or "surprises" will lead to small changes in opinion. On the other hand, those from the opposition party, particularly at the beginning of an administration, are likely to be heavily influenced by news and eager to respond to new information. As a result, they would likely have a large conditional variance (i.e., a weak prior) and a value for the Kalman gain close to 1. Thus, new information should lead to rapid adjustment in their opinions.

Partisan Information Processing

Much of the evidence for the partisan-nature of political decision-making has emerged from experimental studies of decision-making where researchers have more control over the information to which respondents are exposed and can more readily detect when partisan differences arise. Taber and Lodge (2006) designed an experiment in which individuals are allowed to search for information as they make decisions about political issues. They find that individuals simplify the decision-making environment through biased processing of information. In studying the issues of affirmative action and gun control, they find that individuals rely (to varying degrees) on prior attitudes and incorporate these priors when seeking out and evaluating information. In general, respondents exhibit a "disconfirmation bias," which leads them to heavily discount information that is inconsistent with their current position and to readily accept information that is consistent with their existing views. Likewise, when seeking out information, they tend to latch onto information that is supportive of their current position, suggesting a "confirmation bias" as well. Finally, those with higher levels of political knowledge are more strongly influenced by these biases since their added sophistication makes them better able to resist or "counter-argue" information that is contrary to their current position.

The implications of this selective search for and use of information are that partisans should exhibit different updating behavior depending on who occupies the White House. As the time trends for approval show, at the start of each administration, presidents enjoy robust support from their partisan supporters. Consistent with the theory of motivated reasoning, the updating process for partisan supporters of the president should be heavily influenced by priors, in this case the prior is that the president is performing well. Thus, positive information about the president should have little impact on the level of support shown for the incumbent president since approval is already at a high level. Information that might lower presidential approval, on the other hand, is discounted because of the prior belief that the president will perform well. Overall, this theory suggests that supporters of the president should have stronger priors than those opposed to the president.

Those from the party opposed to the president should have a different updating process. Again, at the start of a new administration, presidents generally enjoy their highest level of approval from those identifying with the out-party. Consistent with the theory of motivated reasoning, supporters of the out-party generally seek out information that will confirm their predisposition that the president will not perform well. Thus, they are responsive to new information, particularly any information that will provide reasons to lower their level of approval. Because they are sensitive to new information, supporters of the out-party have weaker priors and are more willing to update.

These expectations for the updating process for the in-party and out-party are consistent with the findings described in Chapter 3 where supporters of presidents maintained a relatively high level of support, while those from the out-party showed considerable variation in their support of the president, responding to both positive and negative news. These general findings can be refined by more explicitly looking at the use of information by partisan groups.

Economic Evaluations

The utility of the updating model and the role of priors and partisanship can be assessed through the economic evaluations described in Chapter 2. For purposes of examining the economic evaluations over a longer time period, the series is reorganized for evaluations of the in-party and the out-party. The updating model was used to estimate the role of prior information on partisanship from 1989 to 2012. During this time period, unemployment was a much more important indicator of the health of the economy than inflation; therefore, the analysis focuses on the way that supporters of the party in power and the party out of power used unemployment in updating their views of the economy. As expected, unemployment had a significant impact on economic evaluations (for both series, $\beta = .21, p < 0.05$).

The model was first run from 1989 to the end of 2007 to exclude the financial crisis and a subsequent analysis will add it back in and explain its significance.

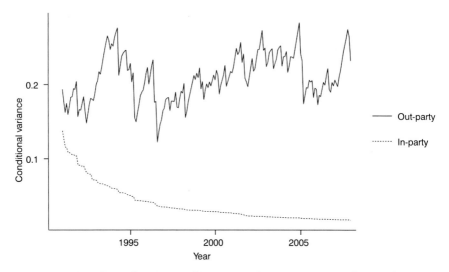

FIGURE 4.3 Conditional variance of in-party and out-party's use of unemployment in updating economic evaluations, 1990–2007

The conditional variance, a measure of the strength of the prior, for both subgroups is reported in Figure 4.3. Consistent with the theory of motivated reasoning, the out-party has a much stronger prior than the in-party, as evident in the larger conditional variance for the out-party. The out-party variance does not quite reach the steady state that the in-party does, meaning that its prior varies across the time period. The calculation of the Kalman gain tells a similar story about the updating behavior of the two groups. The Kalman gain for the in-party stabilizes at 0.85, indicating that about 85 percent of the change in unemployment is used to update the information processing model. In contrast, the Kalman gain for the out-party is nearly 99 percent, meaning the out-party rapidly updates in light of news about the economy.[7]

As noted earlier, at times information is so overwhelming (so precise in the terminology of Bayesian updating) that when it arrives, priors no longer matter. Extending the analysis to include the 2008 financial crisis provides a clear example of this resetting or ignoring of priors. In the analysis through 2012 (shown in the online supplement at http://gemcavoy.wp.uncg.edu/cpr/), the conditional variance for the in-party and the out-party approached zero and the Kalman filter was essentially one for both groups. This means that the priors no longer mattered and that any new information was immediately used to update evaluations of the economy. An alternative way to describe this phenomenon is that the financial crisis led to a regime change, a resetting of all that had come before. The issue of regime changes is examined in depth in the next chapter.

On the whole, this analysis has important implications for our understanding of aggregate opinion. Prior information does play a role in how the public updates its evaluation of the economy as new information emerges. When priors are strong, some new information is discounted, that is updating occurs more slowly than it would during times of uncertainty (as reflected in weak priors or higher conditional variances). These issues are further explored over a longer time period through an analysis of presidential approval.

Approval

Relying on the updating process described for economic ratings, partisan groups can be thought to update their information processing for approval in accordance with new information about inflation and unemployment.[8] Inflation is added to this analysis since it includes the 1970s and 1980s, decades in which concerns about inflation figured prominently in discussions about the strength of the economy. As before, the new information is weighed in the Kalman filter by the conditional variance. From the logic of motivated reasoning, we would expect that the conditional variance for the weight of inflation and unemployment to be higher for the out-party because of their willingness to update in light of new information. In turn, this means that the Kalman gain should be closer to 1 for the out-party since new information leads to updating. The model is estimated separately for in-party approval and out-party approval.

Figure 4.4 shows the Kalman gain for unemployment and inflation on approval for the two partisan groups. For both groups, the weight (or slope) for inflation varies over time, suggesting that both groups use inflation differently over time in updating their views of presidential performance. This change in the role of inflation in the updating process arises from a changing prior or conditional variance (not shown). The conditional variance changes for both groups, but for the in-party the overall variance is generally lower than that for the out-party.[9] The Kalman gain shows a similar pattern, with the in-party using information more than the out-party to update the weight attached to inflation (see Figure 4.4, upper panel). Overall, there is considerable variation in the estimate of the Kalman gain over the whole time period. The 1970s were a particularly turbulent time and both groups altered the weight that they attached to inflation. The 1990s were a more stable period, but the weight changed dramatically again in the 2000s. Both groups reduced the weight that they attached to inflation during the 2000s, but the in-party did so more than the out-party.

The role of unemployment does not show the same time variation as inflation, but nonetheless the role of prior information is evident. Figure 4.4, lower panel, shows that the prior for both partisan groups approach this steady state, but importantly, the steady state arrived at by the in-party is lower than that of the out-party. Again, the in-party updates less in response to new information than the out-party, or, put differently, the in-party has stronger priors than the out-

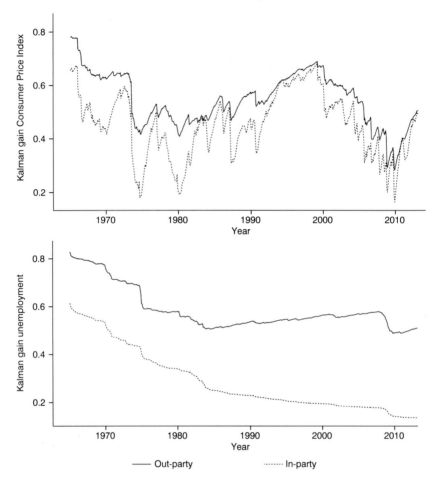

FIGURE 4.4 Kalman gain for partisan updating of unemployment and inflation on presidential approval, 1961–2013

party. The Kalman gain shows a similar pattern in Figure 4.4, lower panel, with the out-party relying more heavily on information about unemployment when updating than the in-party.

The role of partisanship in aggregate economic evaluations is demonstrated in Enns, Kellstedt, and McAvoy (2012) and Enns and McAvoy (2012). This work shows key differences in the way that partisans update their evaluations in light of changes in objective economic indicators, such as unemployment and inflation. Overall, this analysis supports the idea that aggregate behavior is guided by "motivated reasoning" since those supportive of the incumbent president view the economy more positively that those aligned with the out-party, even when controlling for changes in economic conditions.

Information and Reception

Within political science, the impact of economic conditions on public opinion such as presidential approval has been studied extensively. But far less attention has been given to the role of the information processing that underpins these types of analyses.[10] Although much research has been devoted to studying the components of consumer sentiment collected in the Surveys of Consumers, the survey also contains questions about respondents' perceptions of news reports about economic conditions, and these provide insight into the way that people use or ignore relevant information in their assessments of economic conditions.

Although there are a variety of questions asked about the public's awareness of news reports, the focus of the analysis conducted here is on questions about general news about the economy. The question about general news asked in the survey is: "During the last few months, have you heard of any favorable or unfavorable changes in business conditions?" The survey then branches to questions about the type of news heard, focusing on issues like unemployment, inflation, interest rates and a variety of other economic factors. As Soroka and others have shown, there is a negativity bias in news about the economy, since negative information seems to be much more related to people's assessment of the economy than favorable news. The correlations in Table 4.1 show the relationship between the public's rating of the economy (as measured by consumer sentiment), economic conditions, and the news questions. As the table indicates, unfavorable news is more closely related to the public's overall rating of the economy than favorable news. Thus, the focus of the analysis here is on the role of unfavorable news in the public's updating of opinions about the economy.

It is important to note that these simple correlations facilitate our understanding of the public's use of information. The relatively low correlation between favorable news and consumer sentiment indicates that even when the respondents say that they received positive information about the economy, they did not use it systematically in making an overall evaluation of the economy. In addition, the weak correlation between inflation and consumer sentiment indicates that the public is not consistently using information about this inflation in assessing the economy. These weak correlations give support to the idea that the public ignores or is inattentive to some news, focusing its attention on other matters at times.

A times series for this question about news reception is reported in Figure 4.5. As is clear from the figure, there is considerable variation in the public's perception of unfavorable news. The high points correspond with recessions in the early 1990s and 2000s and continue to be high in the wake of the 2008 financial crisis. Low reports of unfavorable news occurred during the second Clinton administration, when the economy was particularly robust.

TABLE 4.1 Correlations among economic ratings, news reception, and economic conditions, 1989–2011

	Consumer sentiment	Unfavorable news	Unemployment	Inflation	Favorable news
Consumer sentiment	1.000	-0.752	-0.636	-0.156	0.196
Unfavorable news	-0.752	1.000	0.457	-0.065	-0.490
Unemploymenty	-0.636	0.457	1.000	-0.287	0.359
Inflation	-0.156	-0.065	-0.287	1.000	-0.302
Favorable news	0.196	-0.490	0.359	-0.302	1.000

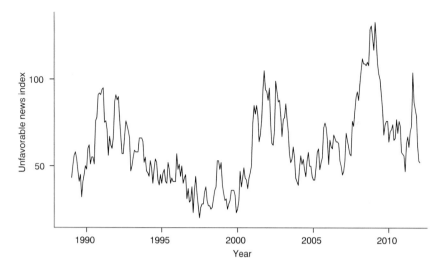

FIGURE 4.5 Hearing unfavorable economic news index, 1989–2012 (source: University of Michigan, Surveys of Consumers, http://press.sca.isr.umich.edu/ accessed May 31 2014)

By looking at relationships between economic conditions and news over time, it is possible to pinpoint more exactly when the public indicates that unfavorable information has been received.[11] Time-varying analysis allows the correlations to change over time and therefore shows the shifting weight in the impact that variables have on each other.

As Figure 4.6 shows, the time-varying relationship indicates that a sharp increase in reception of unfavorable news corresponds with recessions and periods of high unemployment. Thus, during recessions the public is more receptive to unfavorable political news. At first glance this seems an obvious point, but the key is that there is really an interaction between economic conditions and people's perception of economic news. (Interaction here means a change in the slope or the weight of information.) For example, during the middle of the Clinton administration, the impact of changes in unemployment is quite limited, to the point that changes in unemployment have virtually no impact on people's perceptions of economic news. This is in stark contrast to the important, dramatic impact that unemployment has on news reception during recessions.

The results for the time-varying relationship between unfavorable news and inflation indicate that they are not significantly related. In part, this is a byproduct of the time period of the analysis. Inflation was much more volatile in the 1970s and early 1980s than it was after 1989—thus the fact that inflation was relatively stable would likely lead to a limited connection to news reception which varied a lot over time.

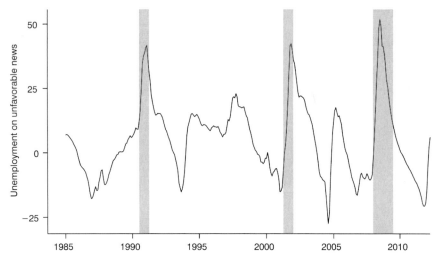

FIGURE 4.6 Time-varying effects of unemployment on news reception, 1985–2012 (gray areas denote recessions)

Although it is useful to uncover the patterns between reception of the news and economic conditions, the key question at hand is the role of economic news in the public's rating of the economy. Based on the analysis above, we would expect to see the impact of information in the economic environment ebb and flow in concert with the amount of news that makes its way to the public, as measured by the news report data. The time-varying relationships for unemployment and inflation are reported in Figure 4.7. It is evident from the figures that there is time variation in the impact of unemployment and inflation on the public's evaluation of the economy as measured by consumer sentiment. The impact of unemployment in economic evaluations is particularly fluid. Periods of recession show that the unemployment rate pulls the public's evaluation of the economy down very dramatically, while between recessions, its impact is fairly minimal. The impact for inflation is also time-varying, but not quite as dramatic as the pattern for unemployment.

Perhaps the most significant finding from this analysis is the correspondence between the time-varying effect for unemployment and the reports about unfavorable news. The plots of unfavorable news (Figure 4.5) and the time-varying effect of unemployment on consumer sentiment (Figure 4.7) look similar and a correlation of the unfavorable news variable and the time-varying parameter for unemployment is a surprisingly high, 0.72. Thus, we can see the effect of receptivity working its way into the public's evaluation of economic conditions through the time-varying effect of unemployment. In other words, the public becomes more receptive to news at important moments, like recessions, and uses that information to update its views of economic conditions.

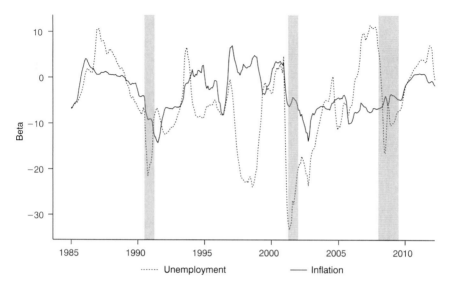

FIGURE 4.7 Time-varying effects of unemployment and inflation on economic evaluations, 1985–2012 (gray areas denote recessions)

As Zaller notes, the availability of information does not necessarily mean that it is received and just because it is received does not mean that it will be used in opinion updating. So unlike theories of rational aggregate behavior which assume that all information that is received will be used, the evidence from this study shows that public is more selective in its use of information. During economic downturns (marked by recessions), there is heightened awareness and use of economic information. During periods of economic prosperity and when other issues are ahead of the economy on the political agenda, the public routinely ignores information that could be useful in updating its assessment of economic conditions. Interestingly, the role of information about economic conditions like unemployment is primarily to drag down the public's assessment of the economy but almost never to increase it. Thus, the public's assessment of economic conditions does not noticeably improve with good news about unemployment.

Conclusion

Bayesian updating has enjoyed renewed attention among those interested in aggregate public opinion particularly with regard to partisanship. There are two features to Bayesian updating that make it useful for the analysis of aggregate public opinion. First, it implies that assessments of political and economic conditions are influenced by the strength or precision of information. In other words, information is weighed in the updating process and weak or imprecise information does not influence new opinions to the extent that precise or "meaningful" information does. Relatedly, the second feature is that prior information about the precision or strength of information matters in updating. New information is filtered through priors so that more dramatic updating will occur when the public has weak priors, for example, at the beginning of a presidential term. Alternatively, when the public or segments of the public have strong priors, new information is not as influential, or is discounted, meaning it will take a steady stream of news to overcome prior information in order to arrive at "updated" opinion. As shown here, partisanship plays a key role in setting priors and influences the dynamics of aggregate opinion, both in evaluations of the economy and performance of the president.

In order to uncover some of the underlying effects of partisanship, this chapter focused on opinion disaggregated by partisan groups. In the next chapter, analysis shifts back to aggregate opinion for the public as a whole (i.e., not disaggregated by partisan groups) in order to examine the role of priors and the use of information in updating aggregate public opinion. In addition, in this chapter's analysis of economic evaluations, we saw that the updating process can undergo regime shifts as in the 2008 financial crisis and that issue is addressed more fully in the next chapter.

The analysis of information and news reception, too, adds to our understanding of the dynamics of aggregate opinion. The public becomes more receptive to news about the economy during difficult times, such as recessions, and uses that information to update its views about economic conditions. Thus, unlike a rational updater who might treat changes in unemployment the same over time, the public takes a more contextual approach. Information is treated differently depending on the situation and this leads to an information-processing model that must incorporate these changes over time and this issue too is addressed more fully in Chapter 6.

Appendix: The Variance Calculation in the Kalman Filter

The first variance term in the numerator of the Kalman gain is P_{t-1}, the sum of the prior estimates of the prediction error variance from 1 to $t-1$. The second variance term, σ_ω^2, can be thought of as underlying changes in "true" opinion arising from changes in the political and economic environment or more generally the uncertainty of x_t. The denominator takes this same sum and adds to it the error in the measurement equation (sampling error plus other errors from voter ignorance, information flow, or the mechanics of survey data collection) and together these provide a measure of the uncertainty associated with random shocks in public opinion. Together, these variances constitute the conditional variances that determine the strengthen or precision of prior information. As the Kalman gain changes, it alters the weight that is given to the prediction error. When the Kalman gain is close to one, most of the variance arises from uncertainty about the x_t's and the prediction error is given full weight (i.e. we are in turbulent times and underlying opinion appears to be moving from time period to time period). If the prediction error is large and the Kalman gain is close to one, the parameters will take a dramatic shift. If the Kalman gain is small, the xs have minimal variance relative to the random error in the model, and the new information (as measured by the prediction error) has minimal impact.

According to Kim and Nelson (1999, 25), the Kalman gain can be re-written as

$$K_t = \frac{1}{x_t} \frac{P_{t|t-1}x_t^2}{P_{t|t-1}x_t^2 + R}$$

In this setup, $P_{t|t-1}x_t^2$ represents the uncertainty associated with the weight of unemployment, $\beta_t \mid \beta_{t-1}$ and R is the uncertainty associated with random shocks to the model, represented by ε_t. Thus, when there is a high level of uncertainty arising from random errors (captured by the prediction error) relative to the uncertainty associated with β_t, then the weight K will go to zero, meaning that there will be little updating to β_t. When the random errors are small relative to the uncertainty in β_t, K will approach 1 and β_t will change in response to prediction errors, trying to reduce future prediction errors.

The estimate of $P_{t|t-1}x_t^2$, the conditional variance, can be thought of as the "prior" in a Bayesian updating model. When it there is a lot of uncertainty the appropriate weight to attach to information about a factor like unemployment, the variance, $P_{t|t-1}x_t^2$, will be relatively large, indicating this uncertainty and new information will be incorporated into the updating equation (and K will approach 1). When there is a strong prior, $P_{t|t-1}x_t^2$ will be smaller and new information will receive less weight (K will move away from 1 towards 0).

If we treat the slope coefficient as the weight assigned to observed information, using unemployment in this case, we want to know how this weight is updated over time to understand how information is being process. The updating equation is:

$$\beta_t = \beta_{t-1} + K_t \eta_{t|t-1}$$

Thus, the current value of β_t is described as a weighted average of $\beta_t \mid \beta_{t-1}$ and the additional information that is carried in the prediction error, $\eta_{t|t-1}$. The gain, K_t, is the weight that is assigned to new information.

Notes

1. The key insight (and one source of controversy) is that it is a theorem of inverse probability. The question for inverse probability is: given the data, what is the probability that my model (or hypothesis) is correct. For example, given that I voted for a Democrat in the last five elections (the observed data), what is the probability that I am a Democrat. The traditional (or frequentist) approach is to specify a model and see if the data are consistent with the model. For example, a frequentist would ask, given that I am a Democrat, what is the probability that I would have voted for a Democrat in the last five presidential elections. In order to calculate the inverse probability, it is necessary to include a prior that specifies the form and strength of prior information.

2. In the world of time series analysis (the method of data analysis upon which this book relies), research described as Bayesian may invoke Bayes' theorem to describe the logic of a model or it may refer to the methods used to estimate a model's parameters.

3. Petris and Petrone (2009, 3) also characterize Bayes' theorem as "formalizing the inductive learning process," by which they mean that people use information to refine an existing theory (their priors). New information does not generally lead to a wholesale reformulation of a theory. However, when the new information is so profound, it can.

4. This example draws upon Albert (2009, 23–25) and Figures 4.1(a) and 4.1(b) are based on his R package, LearnBayes.

5. In a similar vein, Bullock (2009, 1119) describes about how the invasion of Pearl Harbor meant that members of Congress who had been debating the America's entry into World War II received a message with low variance and thus all prior information was irrelevant to future assessments of the benefit of declaring war.

6. The figure with the priors is available in the online supplement at http://gemcavoy. wp.uncg.edu/cpr/. The priors for the this type of analysis can take a variety of forms, from diffuse to informed.

7. These estimates are likely to be a little high because, as noted in Chapter 2, the data are filtered as part of the process of filling in for missing data. An additional analysis of the Bush administration with raw (unfiltered) data, suggests that use of information about unemployment is closer to 43 percent for the in-party and 53 percent for the out-party. This analysis of the unfiltered data was only feasible for the Bush administration because it has the smallest amount of missing data.

8. The estimated model includes dummy variables for transitions and key events.

9. The conditional variance is included in the online supplement http://gemcavoy. wp.uncg.edu/cpr/. I used the Kalman gain in this analysis since it showed the patterns for inflation a little clearer than the conditional variance. In the analysis of economic conditions above, the conditional variance was a little clearer. But, since the Kalman gain is based on the conditional variance, they will always show the same changes in the weight of a variable.

10. Some notable exceptions are Soroka (2006) and De Boef and Kellstedt (2004) who look at the role of media reports on economic evaluations. Erikson, MacKuen, and Stimson (2002) also look at the same perceptions of news reports from the Surveys of Consumers.

11. For these time-varying relationships, I use rolling regressions with a 30-month window. It is possible to estimate these with a time-varying parameter model but since the point of the analysis is simply to show that information reception varies over time, I have used the simpler and more straightforward method, rolling regressions. Time-varying regression parameters are explained more fully in the next chapter.

Bibliography

Albert, Jim. 2009. *Bayesian Computation with R*. New York: Springer Science.

Bartels, Larry. 2002. "Beyond the Running Tally: Partisan Bias in Political Perceptions." *Political Behavior* 24(2):117–150.

Bullock, John G. 2009. "Partisan Bias and the Bayesian Ideal in the Study of Public Opinion." *Journal of Politics* 71(3):1109–1124.

De Boef, Suzanna & Paul M. Kellstedt. 2004. "The Political (and Economic) Origins of Consumer Confidence." *American Journal of Political Science* 48(4):633–649.

Enns, Peter. K. & Gregory E. McAvoy. 2012. "The Role of Partisanship in Aggregate Opinion." *Political Behavior* 34(4):627–651.

Enns, Peter K., Paul M. Kellstedt & Gregory E. McAvoy. 2012. "The Consequences of Partisanship in Economic Perceptions." *Public Opinion Quarterly* 76(2):287–310.

Erikson, Robert S., Michael B. MacKuen & James A. Stimson. 2002. *The Macro Polity*. New York: Cambridge University Press.

Gaines, Brian J., James H. Kuklinski, Paul J. Quirk, Buddy Peyton & Jay Verkuilen. 2007. "Same Facts, Different Interpretations: Partisan Motivation and Opinion on Iraq." *Journal of Politics* 69(4):957–974.

Gelman, Andrew, John B. Carlin, Hal S. Stern, David B. Dunson, Aki Vehtari & Donald B. Rubin. 2013. *Bayesian Data Analysis*. 3rd edition. Boca Raton, FL: Chapman & Hall.

Gerber, Alan & Donald P. Green. 1998. "Rational Learning and Partisan Attitudes." *American Journal of Political Science* 42(3):794–818.

Gill, J. 2007. *Bayesian Methods: A Social and Behavioral Sciences Approach, 2nd edition*. Chapman & Hall/CRC Statistics in the Social and Behavioral Sciences. Boca Raton, FL: CRC Press..

Green, Donald, Bradley Palmquist & Eric Schickler. 2002. *Partisan Hearts and Minds: Political Parties and the Social Identities of Voters*. New Haven, CT: Yale University Press.

Jackman, Simon. 2009. *Bayesian Analysis for the Social Sciences*. Chichester: Wiley.

Kim, Chang-Jin & Charles R. Nelson. 1999. *State-Space Models with Regime Switching: Classical and Gibbs-Sampling Approaches with Applications*. Cambridge, MA: MIT Press.

Kim, Sung-youn, Charles S. Taber & Milton Lodge. 2010. "A Computational Model of the Citizen as Motivated Reasoner: Modeling the Dynamics of the 2000 Presidential Election." *Political Behavior* 32(1):1–28.

Petris, Giovanni & Sonia Petrone. 2009. *Dynamic Linear Models With R*. New York: Springer-Verlag.

Soroka, Stuart N. 2006. "Good News and Bad News: Asymmetric Responses to Economic Information." *Journal of Politics* 68(2):372–385.

Taber, Charles S. & Milton Lodge. 2006. "Motivated Skepticism in the Evaluation of Political Beliefs." *American Journal of Political Science* 50(3):755–769.

Wells, Curt. 1996. *The Kalman Filter in Finance*. Boston. MA: Kluwer Academic Publishers.

Zaller, John R. 1992. *The Nature and Origins of Mass Opinion*. New York: Cambridge University

5

SHIFTING REGIMES

The exploration of partisanship and news in the previous chapters suggests an alternative conceptualization of aggregate public opinion. Gone are the rational updaters who are consistently attentive to changes in the information environment, unbiased by partisanship or media framing, and in their place, we have partisans who generally rely on familiar cues and habits to structure their political decision-making. The challenge then is to reassess the dynamics of aggregate opinion without relying on notions of collective rationality in which an attentive public provides the signal and the inattentive public exerts a minimal influence through its unbiased and random errors. The goal instead is to understand the dynamics of aggregate opinion by incorporating the political exigencies of modern democratic life—that is, to build a model of aggregate opinion rooted in partisanship and a limited capacity for information processing.

As the previous chapters demonstrated, the key to merging partisan concerns, public attention, and political contexts into a coherent explanation of the dynamics of aggregate opinion requires an understanding of the role of priors and information processing. To advance this understanding further requires examining whether, when looking at the public as a whole, priors and the information-processing model hold constant or shift as political and economic issues ebb and flow. As the length of time series for key measures of aggregate opinion grows, this issue becomes even more important. As an example, we might expect a different pattern of updating in the highly polarized politics of the twenty-first century than ones in which partisan differences were not as sharp. Shifting political contexts may lead to a resetting of priors as old ways of processing information do not comport with new settings. Situations in which contexts shift and the models that describe them shift gears or reset are characterized as "regime shifts" and examining them in the context of economic evaluations and presidential approval is the focus of this chapter.

Studies of public opinion provide ample reasons to believe that the way that the public weighs new information is likely to change over time. Individual citizens and the public as a whole are looking for ways to make sense of the wealth of information coming their way without exhaustive research. As established in the previous chapters, party plays an essential role in helping to organize information and opinion. However, there is still room for factors outside of party to shape public opinion. One of the most important factors is priming. The media obviously play an important role in priming the public on nearly all issues. With limited space in the case of newspapers and time in the case of broadcast news, the media must choose which issues to emphasize and as Krosnick and Kinder (1990, 510) argue,

> shifts in news media content alter the political importance that the public attaches to the flow of events. … [T]hrough its monopoly over the immediate telling of political history, media possess the power to influence what the public considers and what it ignores.

The way issues are framed once they are on the public agenda, too, can alter the weight that the public attaches to particular issues. For example, in her analysis of gun politics, Goss (2008) argues that the issue of gun control has at times been framed as a crime, a safety, and a child-welfare issue, and each frame changes the way that the public approaches the issue and the information that it weighs in formulating preferences regarding gun policy. Also, as Ladd (2012) contends, the media itself undergoes large structural shifts and these alter the type of information that people receive and the way that they process it. He argues that the more restrained news reporting that characterized the broadcast television news era provided fewer party cues to the public on salient issues, and that the current era, with a mix of broadcast, cable, and online news provides much stronger party cues. These partisan cues in turn alter the way that the public processes this information when formulating opinions about salient issues.

Politicians, too, try strategically to prime and frame issues for the public. As Kernell (1993) documents, presidents use a strategy of "going public" as they try to mobilize support for their policy initiatives when facing a Congress that is resistant to passing them. Likewise, presidents often direct their attention (and the public's as well) to foreign policy issues, particularly when economic conditions are not in their favor (Kernell 1978, Druckman 2004). Jacobs and Shapiro (2000) show that politicians devote considerable energy between elections trying to build public support for their policy positions, rather than trying to respond to the public's current preferences.

This idea that the public shifts the way that it updates in light of new information is consistent with the idea of learning, that is applying new rules to link information in the environment with expressed opinions. As noted above, this learning might arise from the occurrence of unanticipated events, like Hurricane Katrina, or because politicians try to intentionally alter the process. This kind of learning by using information differently over time is often associated with bounded rationality. Although models of bounded rationality are familiar to political scientists, for the most part they have been applied to decision models (as in Simon 1957) models of policy making (Lindblom's (1959) notion of muddling through), and some formal models (e.g., Bendor 1995). However, bounded rationality models have been notably absent from studies of macro-politics, an area in which they are particularly well-suited. The assumption of bounded rationality in politics is much more consistent with micro-level theories about how individuals acquire and process political information and use it to form political preferences. They continually update and alter their preferences in response to new information (as in schema theory) and are influenced by political elites and news coverage of events (Zaller 1992).

There are two principal ways to approach the study of shifting contexts in public opinion. Both methods are related to state-space methods described earlier, but diverge in their underlying assumptions about the nature of the variation. The first method for estimating this type of relationship is a time-varying parameter (TVP) model and this approach was introduced in the discussion of information processing in Chapter 4. As in a standard regression, the goal is to explain the movement of public opinion using independent variables that track changes in opinion but to relax the assumption that the relationship is constant over time. In this case, the time variation can evolve slowly, shift rapidly, or take periodic jumps. In practice, the TVP method seems to work more effectively in the first two cases (Park 2010). The second approach to studying time variation, changepoint analysis, works more effectively in this middle range where the changes that occur are often abrupt and enduring. These are often described as regime shifts, a name which helps signal both a departure from the past and an enduring quality to the changes.

The TVP model and the changepoint model imply different assumptions about the way that the public updates in the face of new information. The TVP model assumes that the public is attentive to new information in the socio-political environment, but weighs that information based on priors. This type of attentiveness leads to either slow, evolutionary change or rapid changes, depending on the type of information that is relied upon for updating opinion. If the information changes slowly, updating should slowly evolve as well. If information changes rapidly, this should lead to rapid shifts in the weight that information has on the updating behavior of the public. Alternatively, the assumptions of the changepoint model are that public opinion enter periods of relative stability (i.e., the public relies on habits), but these periods of stability are periodically disrupted by events or systemic change in the environment. These disruptions lead to a new information processing model in which the weight attached to information shifts. Another way to think of the changepoint approach is to assume that the public "settles in" on one model or set of weights and these prevail until a significant event or change leads to a revised model, and this process continues over time.

In what follows, I focus on collective opinion as a whole, that is without disaggregating by party. The analysis of aggregate opinion up to this point has stressed the importance of partisan groups and their contribution to the "signal" in aggregate opinion. However, investigating aggregate opinion for the public as a whole means that these two partisan signals are "merged." How this integration of the two signals occurs is not always predictable. In other words, the regimes that emerge for the public as a whole may not be predictable from the changes evident at the partisan group level. However, it is still possible to compare across regimes and better understand the role that partisanship plays in collective opinion.

Time-Varying Parameters—Economic Evaluations

Because it is the more general approach to assessing time variation in the relationship between politico-economic conditions and aggregate public opinion, I begin with the time-varying parameters model. This requires estimating a model in which the independent variables are allowed to change their impact on the dependent variables. These are generally grounded in state-space models, which can be estimated using maximum likelihood methods or in a Bayesian approach, using Markov Chain Monte Carlo (MCMC) methods.[1]

In the context of evaluations of the economy, the structure of the time-varying parameters model is:

$$y_t = \beta_{0t} + \beta_{1t} Unem_t + \beta_{2t} Infl_t + v_t$$
$$\beta_{0t} = \beta_{0t-1} + \omega_{t0}$$
$$\beta_{1t} = \beta_{1t-1} + \omega_{t1}$$
$$\beta_{2t} = \beta_{2t-1} + \omega_{t2}$$

The assumption in this model is that updating behavior will be captured by changes in β_{0t}. Here, the updating behavior is supplemented by information in the economic environment. Thus, in this model of updating, it is possible for the impact of unemployment and inflation to change over time and this effect is captured through the time-varying parameters (β_{1t}, β_{2t}). We would expect this variation to be closely linked to changes in the public's receptivity to news reports.[2]

TABLE 5.1 Hyperparameters for model for time-varying model of economic evaluations

Error variance	Mean	Low	High
Intercept	0.69	0.52	1.04
Unemployment	1.85	1.37	2.85
Inflation	1.94	1.29	3.56

Low and high indicate the boundaries of the 90 percent credible interval. MCMC was run 2,000 times with 4 chains.

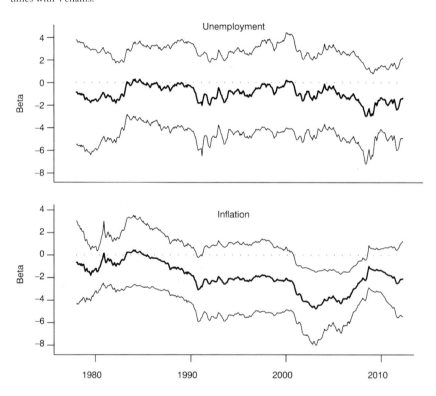

FIGURE 5.1 Time-varying parameters for the impact of economic conditions on evaluations of the economy, 1978–2012. Dark lines represent the time-varying parameter and light lines are the 90 percent credible interval.

The estimation of the TVP model revolves around the variance parameters, the σ_ω^2 and the σ_v^2. If σ_ω^2 goes to zero, this means that there is no variation in the weight of the unemployment or inflation over time and the estimated model is the same as a standard linear regression model, which does not vary over time. If the variances differ from zero, there is meaningful time variation in the parameters. The estimated variances are reported in Table 5.1. As the table shows, the credible intervals do not include zero, therefore there does appear to be meaningful variation in the parameters over time. It is easiest to analyze the time-varying βs in time plots and these are shown in Figure 5.1. As the analysis shows, the estimated impact of unemployment and inflation on economic evaluations is negative, as expected, but the estimates are not especially precise, leading to 90 percent coverage intervals that include zero, raising concerns about the strength of the impact overall. As Park argues, state-space models with time-varying parameters sometimes encounter problems with imprecision because of the difficulty pinning down the true effect when there are few constraints on the model.[3] The substantive implication from this analysis of time-varying parameters is that the public as a whole changes the weight that it attaches to variables like unemployment and inflation when updating, but the updating is likely to be periodic rather than continuous.

Changepoint Model—Economic Evaluations

The changepoint model is an alternative strategy for addressing time variation in parameters and is described by Chib (1998), Park (2010), Spirling (2007), and Western and Kleykamp (2004). In the case of public opinion, the changepoint model suggests that when updating in light of new information, the public as a whole relies on a given model for a while, but when conditions change in significant ways, the model itself is updated as well. The public develops habits or rules of thumb that serve to make sense of the type of information that it is receiving and uses this information to update its evaluation of the economy and presidents. When this information environment changes, either through foreign policy events, domestic crises, economic cycles, etc, the model is updated in concert with these changes.

Researchers often use the idea of regime shifts to talk about deep changes to the context or environment they are studying. In this case, regime changes are associated with dramatic shifts in opinion and the associated changes in the factors that influence it. Some regime shift models focus solely on changes in the dependent variable, but the virtue of the changepoint model used here is that it can also provide estimates of the new weight that the public uses as one regime comes and another goes.[4] Although the estimation of the changepoint models assumes that each regime is different, it is possible to reclassify two or more regimes that are estimated as really two manifestations of the same regime. For example, we might expect economic evaluations to follow the cyclical fluctuations of the business cycle, thus the relationship between economic outcomes and the public's evaluation of the economy might look similar during different periods of economic decline, with unemployment and inflation having similar impacts during recessions. Likewise, during periods of expansion, the weight of these key economic variables might be the same across regimes.

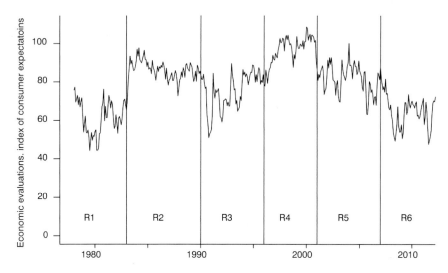

FIGURE 5.2 Economic evaluations (consumer expectations), 1978–2012. R1–6 delineate the estimated regimes (source: Surveys of Consumers, Survey Research Center, University of Michigan).

Given their prominence in discussions of economic conditions, the two key factors influencing economic evaluations are unemployment and inflation.[5] The basic changepoint model is:

$$Econ.Eval_t = \beta_{1i} \times Unemployment_t + \beta_{2i} Inflation_t + \varepsilon_i$$

where i presents the number of regimes. Thus, the influence of unemployment and inflation is specified to be fixed within a regime but can vary across them. In addition, the model estimates the standard error for each regime, making it feasible to identify which regimes experience greatest uncertainty or volatility.[6]

The estimated regimes for the changepoint model for consumer expectations are reported in Figure 5.2. There are a total of six regimes, but not all of them are distinct. As noted earlier, there may be conditions, like recessions, that lead the public to shift the weight it attaches to key economic variables. These weights may shift after the recession and return again the next time the economy experiences a recession. The number of regimes is determined by comparing models with a varying number of regimes and determining which number is "best." Bayes factors are calculated for each of the models, making it possible to determine the probability that one of the models is more likely than the others (Gelman et al. 2013, 182). Included in the analysis is the baseline model in which no changepoints are estimated (that is, a no regime change model). Since the Bayes factors analysis indicates the six-regime model is more probable, given the data, than the no regime change model (and all others as well), the changepoint model is an improvement over the standard linear regression model that does not account for regime changes.

The first regime runs from January 1978, the start of the series, to March 1983. This regime encompasses some of the most turbulent economic conditions in the postwar era. The regime includes the 1979 oil crisis that developed in the wake of the Iranian Revolution and the dramatic decline in Iranian oil production that followed. This occurred in the midst of the stagflation that had gripped the economy during the mid-1970s and continued into the early 1980s. In response to these conditions, the Federal Reserve, under the leadership of Paul Volcker, implemented tight monetary policy aimed at slowing down the economy and purging inflationary expectations. In the end, Fed policy succeeded in its goal to end stagflation, but came at the price of record high interest rates and unemployment. The second regime begins with a spike in the public's optimism about the economy. As the figure shows, this spike is followed by a period of steady optimism about economic conditions that runs from 1983 to the middle of 1990. The third regime is notable for its volatility as the public's view of the economy shifts repeatedly until the middle of 1996. The volatility of economic evaluations from 1990 to 1996 is not surprising since this time period included the invasion of Kuwait by Saddam Hussein and the Iraqi army, the recession of 1990–91, and ongoing concerns about the federal deficit. This period of volatility is followed by a regime defined by the unprecedentedly high economic evaluations that arose during the second half of the 1990s, a time period that includes the longest economic expansion of the postwar era. The optimism of the 1990s gave way to two different periods of economic contraction. The first began about the time that President George W. Bush took office in 2001 and the decline accelerated after the terrorist attacks of 9/11. This regime lingered on until the economy declined further starting in 2008, marking the start of the final regime. Interestingly, the onset of this regime shows that the public's assessment of the economy shifted downward prior to the financial meltdown that became a crisis in October 2008. This regime remained in place into 2012, the end of the time period for this study. The only regime characterized solely by an economic expansion occurred during the "boom" years of the 1990s, when both the stock market and the economy reached new highs (regime 4). The other regimes were defined either by periods of uncertainty or economic turmoil.

The different regimes estimated from the data successfully identify periods when the dynamics of the public's evaluation of the economy change and make it feasible to see if the role of news and information changes as these regimes shift. In some ways it would be surprising if the weight of news and information did not shift along with large changes in economic evaluations. But, this can only be established with some confidence by assessing the impact of key variables like unemployment and inflation during each regime. The

TABLE 5.2 Time frame for the estimated regimes from the changepoint model for economic evaluations

Regime	Start (year, month)	End (year, month)
1	1978, 1	1983, 2
2	1983, 3	1990, 6
3	1990, 7	1996, 6
4	1996, 7	2001, 1
5	2001, 2	2007, 12
6	2008, 1	—

impact of economic factors during these regimes is reported in Table 5.3. As the table shows, across these regimes, the impact of unemployment and inflation changed as the public revised the weight that it attached to each factor in its assessment of the economy, and at various times, the weight of one or the other factor fell to zero. This means that at times either unemployment or inflation essentially "turn off" and play no role in how the public updates its assessment of the economy. In none of the regimes did both unemployment and inflation become insignificant at the same time, and this shows that the public is always using some economic information to update its evaluation of the economy.[7]

As Table 5.3 shows, the impact of unemployment and inflation shifts in both its weight and how precisely it is estimated.[8] The first regime (starting in 1978) has the most precise estimate for both inflation and unemployment (as evident by the smallest standard deviation), indicating that the impact of unemployment and inflation on economic evaluations was fairly consistent in each of the months included in it. But the weight of these variables on economic evaluations was not as great as in other regimes. Inflation had the highest weight (–0.344) during the early 2000s and unemployment had its highest weight during the economic expansion of the Clinton administration (–0.420 in regime 3 and –0.527 in regime 4).[9] The weight of inflation was a little more consistent across the regimes than unemployment. Also at times, the intervals include zero, meaning it is unlikely that the variable had an impact on economic evaluations during that regime. During the 2008 financial crisis, both unemployment and inflation played a role in people's evaluations of the economy.

The important finding from this analysis is that the impact of economic conditions will shift over time as the public adapts to changing circumstances, information, and cues so that the weight of these factors varies over time. Across these regimes, the impact of unemployment and inflation shifted as the public revised the weight that it attached to these factors in its assessment of the economy, and at various times, the weight of these factors fell to zero. As noted above, this

TABLE 5.3   Changepoint model for economic evaluations

Independent variable: inflation

	Regime	Coefficient	Standard deviation	Low	High
1	1978, 1	−0.197	0.024	−0.238	−0.157
2	1983, 3	0.104	0.047	0.025	0.181
3	1990, 7	−0.228	0.062	−0.328	−0.124
4	1996, 7	−0.149	0.081	−0.283	−0.014
5	2001, 2	−0.344	0.072	−0.461	−0.223
6	2008, 1	−0.116	0.049	−0.199	−0.037

Independent variable: unemployment

	Regime	Coefficient	Standard deviation	Low	High
1	1978, 1	−0.016	0.053	−0.103	0.072
2	1983, 3	0.227	0.060	0.128	0.324
3	1990, 7	−0.420	0.079	−0.547	−0.285
4	1996, 7	−0.527	0.089	−0.669	−0.376
5	2001, 2	0.074	0.104	−0.097	0.246
6	2008, 1	−0.102	0.041	−0.169	−0.035

Error variance

	Regime	σ^2	Standard deviation	Low	High
1	1973,1	0.412	0.068	0.314	0.536
2	1983, 3	0.130	0.025	0.095	0.175
3	1990, 7	0.334	0.058	0.252	0.438
4	1996, 7	0.233	0.040	0.175	0.305
5	2001, 2	0.239	0.041	0.180	0.312
6	2008, 1	0.364	0.067	0.270	0.486

Low and high indicate the boundaries of the 90 percent credible interval. MCMC chains were run 10,000 times after discarding the first 2,000.

means that the public was not using this variable in its updating at all, and this is an important difference from the standard approach that assumes the impact of variables is the same across time and that information will not be ignored. The regimes also exhibit different levels of volatility, with some quiescent and others tumultuous. In addition, the changing role of unemployment and inflation is consistent with the overall view developed here, that the impact of economic factors is not constant over time and the public relies on different models in its evaluation of the economy depending on the context.[10]

Given earlier evidence of the significant role of partisanship in the dynamics of aggregate opinion, it is important to consider its influence across regimes. There does appear to be a trend in the role that economic indicators play in overall economic evaluations and it is a diminishing one. In the later years, those associated with higher partisanship and more partisan bias, the impact of unemployment and inflation is generally declining, with small weights in the last regime that started in 2008. This is consistent with the idea that extreme partisanship weakens the link between economic conditions and evaluations (Druckman, Peterson & Slothuus 2013).

The analysis of economic evaluations demonstrates one of the key themes in this book—namely, that the public is sensitive to changes in context when making judgments about economic conditions, but these changes are not continuous. Instead, we observe that the public develops "habits" that it uses over time, but that these habits are periodically replaced as noteworthy changes in the economic environment occur and require the public to revise the way that it links changes in the environment to assessments about economic conditions.

Time-Varying Parameters—Presidential Approval

For an analysis of presidential approval, it is worth going back to first principles and examine whether changes in the political and economic environment lead to constant or periodic changes in the way that the public updates in light of new information. Given that presidential approval falls more clearly in the category of a valence issue, it is possible there would be more fluidity in the role of information over time. As numerous studies have demonstrated, presidential approval can change in response to economic conditions, events, and elections. Thus, it is possible that the change in this context is continuous rather than periodic. On the other hand, given that continuous updating requires more consistent monitoring of information in the environment and the cognitive demands that this places on citizens, it is possible, even likely, that the periodic updating evident in economic evaluations will be apparent in this domain as well. Thus, it makes sense to begin the analysis with an examination of the full time-varying parameter model and then to turn to the changepoint model.

Several theories of presidential politics provide a rationale for changing parameters as a result of shifting political contexts. In analyzing presidential approval, there are two ways in which the parameters can shift, either within an administration or across administrations. Focusing first on shifts within administrations, Alesina and Rosenthal (1995) and Alesina, Roubini, and Cohen (1997) develop a model of rational partisanship to explain why parties pursue different economic outcomes. The model describes the variation in the influence that presidents have on economic policy over the course of their administration. According to this model, presidents are able to influence economic outcomes in their preferred direction in the first two years of their administration, and then there is a return to normal outcomes after that. The public may use a similar timeframe in thinking about the impact of the president on economic policy. In the first two years, expectations are relatively high and there is a close link between expectations and approval. However, later in the administration, the public may believe that presidents have altered economic outcomes to the extent that they can, given the difficulties of passing economic reform legislation. Light (1998) provides a similar argument about presidents' influence over the course of their administration. His argument is that presidents have political capital early in their administration because they have recently won an election and are popular. However, in order to get legislation passed, they must spend their political capital and are therefore less influential later in their administration. In addition, the public may see presidents as more responsible for the economy early in their administration and once this initial period of high influence has passed, they are viewed as less responsible. This can lead to changes within regimes in the importance that the public attaches to information in the environment.

The second type of parameter variation is across administrations. Presidential scholars have argued that the New Deal and the Keynesian economic management associated with it led to growing expectations that modern presidents are responsible for macro-economic outcomes (see for example, Edwards & Wayne 1990). However, there are competing theories that the president's influence on economic outcomes is diminishing. Others have argued that the Fed has become the dominant economic policymaker because of fears that the stagflation of the 1970s will return (Greider 1987). And, finally, there is a general sense that politics has thickened due to the complexity of federal programs and the mobilization of special interests, and these developments have limited the influence of presidents over policy (Skowronek 1993). If the public changes its expectations in response to these changes in context, this will lead to a change in the weight attached to economic and political news.

In addition, as noted at the outset of this chapter, the shifting focus of the media onto and away from issues can influence the importance that the public attaches to incoming information. Presidents, too, at times try to alter the way that the public evaluates them by strategically emphasizing issues in which they are likely to be viewed favorably and masking ones that are working against them. This priming of issues by presidents and the media can influence the weight that is attached to information over time (Druckman 2004).

As noted before, the time-varying parameters model requires estimating the variances of the βs and plotting the impact of variables over time, as shown in Figure 5.3.[11] The model was estimated with consumer expectations as an

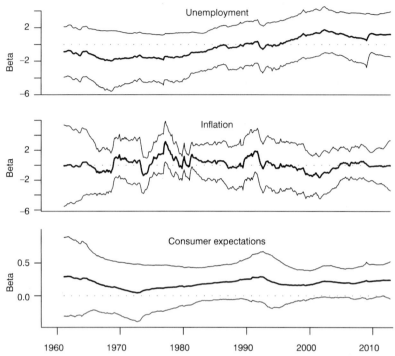

FIGURE 5.3 Time-varying parameters for the impact of economic factors on presidential approval, 1961–2012. Dark lines represent the time-varying parameter and light lines are the 90 percent credible interval

independent variable as well. The time-varying parameter for consumer expectations had a much smaller range than those for inflation and unemployment. Like the parameters for unemployment and inflation in the analysis of economic evaluations, it varied over time, but lacked the precision that sometimes occurs with this type of time-varying analysis.[12]

The impact of inflation and unemployment on presidential approval from 1961–2012 is reported in Figure 5.3. As the figure shows, the impact of these variables shifts over time, and these changes are consistent with the idea that different contexts and time periods lead the public to alter how it uses factors like unemployment and inflation in its evaluation of presidential approval. In Table 5.4, the estimates of the variances for the time-varying parameters show that there is meaningful time variation in the parameters, since the 90 percent credible intervals for the variance parameters do not include zero. But the figure also shows that the estimates lack precision overall, since the error bands in Figure 5.3 include zero for the most part. Thus, the overall findings suggest that time variation in the impact of these variables exists, but the time-varying parameter model does not precisely capture its impact. As was the case with

TABLE 5.4 Hyperparameters for model for time-varying model of presidential approval

Error variance	Mean	Standard deviation	Low	High
Intercept	2.54	0.69	1.96	4.20
Unemployment	8.81	2.78	5.42	15.28
Inflation	4.90	0.49	4.35	5.93
Consumer expectations	8.60	3.79	3.95	15.06

Note: Low and high indicate the boundaries of the 90 percent credible interval. MCMC was run 2,000 time with 4 chains.

the public's evaluation of the economy, this imprecision might arise from an updating process that is marked by abrupt changes, consistent with the shifting regimes of a changepoint model.

Changepoint Model—Presidential Approval

The literature on presidential approval has established three sets of factors that influence presidential approval: events, economic conditions, and elections. The economic factors included in the changepoint model for approval are inflation, unemployment, and consumer expectations. For events, I rely on the list of events described by Newman and Forcehimes (2010). These are aggregated into categories of positive and negative events for both domestic and international issues. The model also includes indicators of presidential transitions, with the first month of a presidential transition coded 1 and the others 0. As Park (2010) suggests, for changepoint models this approach of using an exogenous event like an election in the model may lead to a regime shift, but does not arbitrarily limit the length of the regime change. Also, not all presidential transitions lead to regime changes. For example, the transfer of the presidency from George H.W. Bush to Bill Clinton did not produce a dramatic change in presidential approval. At the time of the transition, Bush had regained some of the popularity that he had lost during the election year of 1992, and Clinton did not have particularly high approval early in his administration when compared to other presidents.

Estimates of the changepoint model identified eight regimes. The eight regime model is determined by estimating models with no changepoints and models with one through nine changepoints. The baseline model of "no changepoints" plays an important role in this analysis. It serves as a comparison of the traditional approach to analyzing presidential approval (i.e., no regime shifts, other than presidential transitions) and the changepoint approach that does not restrict the number of regimes to one. The Bayes factors analysis provides a means to test whether the changepoint model outperforms the

TABLE 5.5 Time frame for the estimated regimes from the changepoint model for presidential approval

Regime	Start (year, month)	End (year, month)
1	1961, 2	1968, 12
2	1969, 1	1974, 7
3	1974, 8	1980, 12
4	1981, 1	1986, 11
5	1986, 12	1991, 12
6	1992, 1	2000, 5
7	2000, 6	2006, 9
8	2006, 10	—

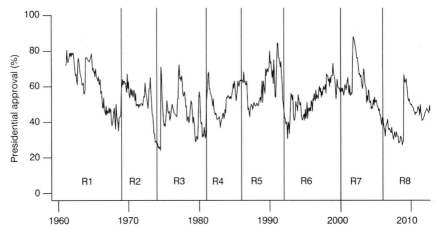

FIGURE 5.4 Presidential approval with estimated regimes, 1961–2012. R1–8 delineate the estimated regimes.

standard regression model. If the analysis of the Bayes factors shows that models with regime shifts have a higher probability of fitting the data, then there is reason to believe that the dynamics of presidential approval periodically shift. And, indeed, the analysis does indicate that multiple regimes are more likely than the standard model.

The dates for each regime are reported in Table 5.5.

Table 5.6 provides estimates of the coefficients for economic variables and how their impact shifted with regimes.[13] Across the regimes, the changepoint model shows that increases in inflation leads to lower presidential approval, as expected. Its impact is fairly consistent but as seen in Table 5.6, there are two groupings of the coefficients, one group with a higher mean (Regimes 1,6, and 7) centered on –0.4 and the second with a lower mean, but narrower distribution. In other words, even though inflation consistently influences presidential approval, it has more impact at some times than others. The impact of consumer expectations, too, varies over time, with a large, positive impact in the first regime (covering the 1960s) and a smaller positive impact for most of the other regimes. A few of the estimates of the impact of consumer expectations on presidential approval have coverage intervals that include zero, so we cannot be fully confident of the impact of consumer expectations for those regimes. The results for unemployment, too, vary over time, and are mostly in line with the theoretical expectation that increases in unemployment lead to lower presidential approval. What is most notable from the analysis is the uncertain connection between unemployment and approval in the last two regimes. For much of George W. Bush's presidency, foreign policy concerns dominated the political agenda and this might explain the generally weak link between unemployment and approval under regime 7. President Obama, on the other hand, came into office with a very high approval rating and high unemployment. So again it is not too surprising that changes in unemployment do not track changes in approval particularly closely. This negative finding, i.e., the absence of a correlation between unemployment and approval, is important to our understanding of the way the public uses information about the economy: at times, important information about the economy is ignored.

In addition, given a prevailing sense that politics of the 2000s is manifestly different from earlier time periods (particularly with regard to elite partisanship and political polarization—Druckman, Peterson & Slothuus 2013, Jacobson 2006, Levendusky 2009), this finding bears further investigation. From Figure 5.4, there are similarities in the dynamics of regime 1 and regimes 7 and 8. Both are trending down and cover a similar range in the approval ratings. In addition, Table 5.6 includes the error variance for each regime, an indicator of the size of the errors in the estimation, and they are similar for these regimes. This means that the variables in the model do about the same at explaining the variation in approval across regimes. But, in general, the impact of unemployment, inflation and consumer expectations is larger in the 1960s than in the 2000s, and unemployment, as noted above, does not seem to have a meaningful impact on approval in the 2000s. Although a full explanation of these differences requires more analysis than can be done here, they are consistent with the idea that periods of high partisanship are associated with a weaker correspondence between economic indicators and expressed opinion.[14]

By re-running the analysis for these two time periods (the 1960s and the 2000s) and calculating the Kalman gain for the information-processing model, the use of information in the two regimes can be compared. The Kalman gain for unemployment and inflation reached a steady state in each regime, so they are not plotted over time. For both unemployment and inflation, the use of economic news by the public as a whole was much higher in the 1960s than

TABLE 5.6 Changepoint model for presidential approval

Independent variable: unemployment / *Inflation*

	Regime	Coefficient	Standard deviation	Low	High	Coefficient	Standard deviation	Low	High
1	1961, 2	-0.185	0.141	-0.415	0.047	-0.370	0.121	-0.567	-0.173
2	1969, 1	-0.044	0.078	-0.171	0.086	-0.184	0.052	-0.270	-0.098
3	1974, 8	0.019	0.100	-0.147	0.181	-0.125	0.054	-0.215	-0.037
4	1981, 1	-0.274	0.058	-0.370	-0.178	-0.052	0.027	-0.097	-0.006
5	1986, 12	-0.138	0.099	-0.299	0.025	0.274	0.078	0.147	0.402
6	1992, 1	-0.143	0.095	-0.299	0.014	-0.429	0.131	-0.647	-0.213
7	2000, 6	0.315	0.108	0.136	0.493	-0.401	0.114	-0.589	-0.212
8	2006, 10	0.083	0.075	-0.043	0.206	-0.173	0.041	-0.241	-0.107

Consumer expectations / *Error variance (σ^2)*

	Regime	Coefficient	Standard deviation	Low	High	Coefficient	Standard deviation	Low	High
1	1961, 2	0.048	0.011	0.030	0.066	0.231	0.036	0.178	0.297
2	1969, 1	-0.007	0.009	-0.022	0.007	0.353	0.063	0.263	0.465
3	1974, 8	0.014	0.011	-0.005	0.033	0.572	0.103	0.427	0.759
4	1981, 1	0.012	0.006	0.002	0.022	0.339	0.061	0.252	0.448
5	1986, 12	0.013	0.008	0.000	0.026	0.745	0.115	0.576	0.948
6	1992, 1	0.021	0.006	0.012	0.031	0.190	0.032	0.145	0.247
7	2000, 6	0.001	0.007	-0.010	0.012	0.290	0.053	0.214	0.388
8	2006, 10	0.015	0.006	0.004	0.025	0.254	0.039	0.197	0.323

Note: Low and high indicate the boundaries of the 90 percent credible interval. MCMC chains were run 10,000 times after discarding the first 2,000.

the 2000s. In the 1960s, the Kalman gain for unemployment was 0.90 and for inflation it was 0.73. (Again, a higher Kalman gain means greater use of information in updating, or less reliance on priors.) By contrast, in the 2000s, the calculation for unemployment was 0.81 and for inflation it was 0.21. The difference in the use of inflation in updating is not too surprising, since inflation has not been a big concern in recent years. The 10 percentage point drop in the weight of unemployment is especially noteworthy, since so much attention has been placed on it as an indicator of overall economic well-being. It is difficult to pin down precisely how much of this erosion of the influence of these variables is due to heightened partisanship. However, based on the analysis in the last chapter, there was a big difference between partisans in their use of unemployment in the updating model, especially in recent years where the out-party incorporated about 60 percent of information about unemployment into its updates and the in-party used about 20 percent.[15]

Conclusion

The key finding in this chapter is that the dynamics of both presidential approval and economic evaluations are more effectively captured by the changepoint model than the TVP model. From this, we learn that the way that the public as a whole processes information is not constant across time. Instead, the public relies on rules of thumb or "habits" in connecting information in the environment to its views about presidents and the economy.[16] These rules of thumb are relied upon for a while, but when circumstances change, the public alters the way that it uses information.[17]

We know that there are a variety of other reasons to expect the public to update the way that it uses information in formulating opinions about presidents and the economy. Priming and framing issues can profoundly influence the way that people use information available to them. In addition, political strategies employed by political elites try to structure the information that people pay attention to as well as how they use that information once they receive it.

These insights corroborate the findings from previous chapters and help to make the case that the dynamics of aggregate opinion cannot be fully explained by a simple signal-and-noise model in which the attentive public provides a consistent framework for relating information in the environment to revised public opinion. Instead, the process is significantly influenced by the political realities of modern democratic life, salience of issues, changing levels of partisan bias, etc. Contexts change and the role that information plays is fluid rather than constant. However, these results require considering, once again, the coherence and legitimacy of aggregate public opinion since the dynamics of public opinion shown here suggest a much more complex use of information than is proposed by an explanation based on an "attentive" and "inattentive" public.

Notes

1. Although both maximum likelihood and MCMC methods will typically yield similar estimates, the interpretation of the MCMC parameters is more consistent with the Bayesian framework outlined here. But it is possible to estimate Bayesian updating models with maximum likelihood methods; in fact, this is the most common approach. Whether maximum likelihood or Bayesian methods are the better approach is a matter of ongoing debate.

   To improve the speed and precision of the estimation, the data for presidential approval and economic evaluations were standardized prior to estimation in order that the variances are of a similar magnitude. In order to have a longer time series for the economic evaluation series, consumer expectations from the Surveys of Consumers is used for the analysis, rather than the merged data used to estimate partisan groups. The merged data begins in 1989, while the Surveys of Consumers begins in 1978.

2. It is possible to incorporate the impact of news directly in the model by specifying news as an explanatory factor in the β_is, but the results of this more complex specification are nearly identical to the one described here.

3. It is important to note, however, that this is not always the case since time-varying effects have been shown to be important in a variety of settings, e.g., Beck (1983), Bond, Fleisher, and Wood (2003), and McAvoy (2006).

4. State-space models with time-varying parameters, like the ones described and analyzed above, can include regime shifts as well (Kim & Nelson 1999), but the same challenge in terms of the precision of the estimated time varying effects arises even when introducing regime shifts, since the model still provides little structure to the time variation. In fact, many of the time-varying parameters reported in Kim and Nelson (1999) are not significant once confidence intervals are included.

5. A measure of overall economic conditions like GDP is likely to also be related to economic evaluations; however, the analysis here relies on monthly data and GDP is measured quarterly. A similar analysis (not shown) to the one presented here was conducted using a proxy for GDP that is available monthly, industrial production. Its addition to the model does not significantly alter the general findings presented here—that is, the same regimes and shifts in the weight of inflation and unemployment are evident.

6. This analysis was conducted using the R package MCMCpack (http://mcmcpack.berkeley.edu/).

7. In the second regime, both unemployment and inflation were positively related to economic evaluations. Even though this was a turbulent time for the economy, further analysis of the model to look for specification errors is needed.

8. In the table, the standard deviation gives a quick sense of which coefficients are measured precisely, as indicated by a small standard deviation. A comparison of the high and low values is a little more difficult when looking at the table, but can be seen in density plots in the online supplement at http://gemcavoy.wp.uncg.edu/cpr/.

9. Since the dependent variables are standardized and have a similar variance, this comparison of coefficient size across regimes makes some sense.

10. Plots of the priors that show how they are reset are available in the online supplement at http://gemcavoy.wp.uncg.edu/cpr/.

11. The time-varying model included control variables for domestic and international events, casualties in the Vietnam war and the war in Iraq, Watergate, the Gulf War.

12. This analysis was conducted using the R package rstan, an R implementation of the Stan program (Stan Development Team 2013). The time-varying model included estimates of an autoregressive conditional heteroskedasticity (ARCH) error term to address heteroskedasticity in the residuals.

13. The impact of positive and negative news events and the dummy variables are not reported in the table.
14. This is examined experimentally by Druckman, Peterson, and Slothuus (2013).
15. By combining estimates from the changepoint model with the Kalman filter, it is possible to show how the priors shift as regimes change for economic evaluations and presidential approval. As each regime begins, there is a lot of uncertainty and the unconditional variance is high, but over time the variance reaches a steady state and there is little to no updating in the parameters. Figures displaying the resetting of priors are in the online supplement at http://gemcavoy.wp.uncg.edu/cpr/.
16. The online supplement for this chapter at http://gemcavoy.wp.uncg.edu/cpr/ shows how the priors for the parameters are reset as each regime begins.
17. MacKuen et al. (2010, 440) contend that people approach politics with two different modes. In one mode, they rationally update in light of new information and set "aside prior commitments and consider novel points of view." In the other mode, they switch to partisan reasoning and emphasize party loyalty and winning political contests in their assessment of political information. The idea that people rely on two modes when making judgments is described in general terms in Kahneman (2011), but MacKuen et al. (2010) show how it works in political deliberation. Their argument about individuals is consistent with the changepoint analysis presented here, and this suggests that the public as well as individuals rely on two modes.

Bibliography

Alesina, Alberto & Howard Rosenthal. 1995. *Partisan Politics, Divided Government, and the Economy.* Cambridge: Cambridge University Press.

Alesina, Alberto, Nouriel Roubini & Gerald D. Cohen. 1997. *Political Cycles and the Macroeconomy.* Cambridge, MA: MIT Press.

Beck, Nathaniel. 1983. "Time-Varying Regression Models." *American Journal of Political Science* 27(3):557–600.

Bendor, Jonathan. 1995. "A Model of Muddling Through." *American Political Science review* 89(4):819–831.

Bond, Jon R., Richard Fleisher & B. Dan Wood. 2003. "The Marginal and Time-Varying Effect of Public Approval on Presidential Success in Congress." *Journal of Politics* 65(1):92–110.

Chib, Siddhartha. 1998. "Estimation and Comparison of Multiple Change-Point Models." *Journal of Econometrics* 86(2):221–241.

Druckman, James N. 2004. "Does Presidential Rhetoric Matter?: Priming and Presidential Approval." *Presidential Studies Quarterly* 34(4):755–779.

Druckman, James N., Erik Peterson & Rune Slothuus. 2013. "How Elite Partisan Polarization Affects Public Opinion Formation." *The American Political Science Review* 107(1):57–79.

Edwards, George C. III & Stephen Wayne. 1990. *Presidential Leadership: Politics and Policymaking.* New York: St. Martin's Press.

Gelman, Andrew, John B. Carlin, Hal S. Stern, David B. Dunson, Aki Vehtari & Donald B. Rubin. 2013. *Bayesian Data Analysis.* 3rd edition. Boca Raton, FL: Chapman & Hall.

Goss, Kristen A. 2008. *Disarmed: The Missing Movement for Gun Control in America.* Princeton, NJ: Princeton University Press.

Greider, William. 1987. *Secrets of the Temple.* New York: Simon & Schuster.

Jacobs, Lawrence R. & Robert Y. Shapiro. 2000. *Politicians Don't Pander: Political Manipulation and the Loss of Democratic Responsiveness.* Chicago, IL: University of Chicago Press.

Jacobson, Gary C. 2006. *Divider, Not a Uniter: George W. Bush and the American People.* New York: Pearson Longman.

Kahneman, Daniel. 2011. *Thinking Fast and Slow.* New York: Macmillan.

Kernell, Samuel. 1978. "Explaining Presidential Popularity." *American Political Science Review* 72:506–522.

Kernell, Samuel. 1993. *Going Public: New Strategies of Presidential Leadership.* Washington, DC: CQ Press.

Kim, Chang-Jin & Charles R. Nelson. 1999. *State-Space Models with Regime Switching: Classical and Gibbs-Sampling Approaches with Applications.* Cambridge, MA: MIT Press.

Krosnick, Jon A. & Donald R. Kinder. 1990. "Altering the Foundations of Support for the President Through Priming." *American Political Science Review* 84(2):497–512.

Ladd, Jonathan M. 2012. *Why Americans Hate the Media and How It Matters.* Princeton, NJ: Princeton University Press.

Levendusky, Matthew. 2009. *The Partisan Sort.* Chicago, IL: University of Chicago Press.

Light, Paul C. 1998. *The President's Agenda: Domestic Policy Choice from Kennedy to Clinton.* 3rd edition. Baltimore, MD: The Johns Hopkins University Press.

Lindblom, Charles. 1959. "The Science of 'Muddling Through'." *Public Administration Review:* 19(2):79–88.

MacKuen, Michael B., Jennifer Wolak, Luke Keele & George E. Marcus. 2010. "Civic Engagements: Resolute Partisanship or Reflective Deliberation." *American Journal of Political Science* 54(2):440–458.

McAvoy, Gregory E. 2006. "Stability and Change: The Time Varying Impact of Economic and Foreign Policy Evaluations on Presidential Approval." *Political Research Quarterly* 59(1):71–83.

Newman, Brian & Andrew Forcehimes. 2010. "Rally Round the Flag Events for Presidential Approval Research." *Electoral Studies* 29(1):144–154.

Park, Jong Hee. 2010. "Structural Change in U.S. Presidents' Use of Force." *American Journal of Political Science* 54(3):766–782.

Simon, Herbert. 1957. *Models of Man: Social and Rational.* New York: Wiley.

Skowronek, Stephen. 1993. *The Politics Presidents Make.* Cambridge, MA: Harvard University Press.

Spirling, Arthur. 2007. "Bayesian Approaches for Limited Dependent Variable Change Point Problems." *Political Analysis* 15(4):387–405.

Stan Development Team. 2013. "Stan: A C++ Library for Probability and Sampling, Version 2.01." http://mc-stan.org

Western, Bruce & Meredith Kleykamp. 2004. "A Bayesian Change Point Model for Historical Time Series Analysis." *Political Analysis* 12(4):354–374.

Zaller, John R. 1992. *The Nature and Origins of Mass Opinion.* New York: Cambridge University Press.

6

THE GOOD-ENOUGH PUBLIC

For a long time, political observers and researchers have been frustrated by the public's inability to measure up to the ideals of democratic citizenship. Among the public's many documented failings are an inability to form coherent preferences, limited factual knowledge about current events and political leaders, and low participation rates in elections. However, aggregate studies of political behavior have tried to restore legitimacy to political decision-making by arguing that although individuals may fail to meet the standards of good democratic citizenship, through the miracle of aggregation and the subset of the public that is attentive, political decision-making can have meaning and legitimacy. The difficulty is that in making this leap from individual irrationality to collective rationality, researchers have side-stepped or ignored some of the key findings from individual-level studies about how the public processes information and the extent to which its ability to process information is compatible with collective rationality.

The Bayesian updating model that I have developed in this book addresses this difficulty. The analysis of aggregate opinion reveals a much more complex relationship between information, news, and opinion than models of strict rationality suggest. The public does process new information and some of it is put to use in updating opinions about presidential performance, economic conditions, attitudes about the environment, and a host of other issues. However, the updating process is not as straightforward as the conventional stimulus-response model would suggest. News about political and economic conditions is weighed in light of prior judgments that incorporate partisan cues, the salience of issues, and shifting political contexts (i.e., regimes). In addition, the certainty or uncertainty associated with new information influences the weight that is attached to it. News in October 2008 about financial institutions such as Lehman Brothers failing leaves little doubt that the economy is in a crisis, whereas there is less certainty about the significance of new reports that the unemployment rate fell from 6.0 percent to 5.8 percent as it did in January 2003.

This alternative form of information processing, one more aligned with the realities of political decision-making, raises questions about the rationality of collective opinion. Does the influence of partisanship, salience (or attention), and regime shifts lead to collective opinion that can be defended as "rational"? As described in the introductory chapter, what is meant by rationality in the context of collective opinion is part of an ongoing debate. Some researchers focus on ideal types or ideal citizens; others use quantitative models to understand whether the public learns from errors or repeats them; and others still compare public opinion to some kind of benchmark to assess the rationality of collective opinion. In this chapter, I provide a novel benchmark as a test of the public's rationality by comparing judgments about the economy by experts to those of the public over time.

For economic evaluations, the quarterly Survey of Professional Forecasters makes a comparison of experts and the public feasible. Administration of the survey began in 1968 by the American Statistical Association, then moved to the National Bureau of Economic Research, and finally in 1990, the Federal Reserve Bank of Philadelphia took control of it. The survey asks economists and professional forecasters working for government and business a battery of questions about current and future economic conditions, including unemployment, inflation, interest rates, etc. Researchers like Carroll (2003) and Mankiw, Reis, and Wolfers (2004) have demonstrated the usefulness of the survey in comparing assessments of inflationary expectations by experts and citizens, but it has not been utilized as a benchmark of overall economic evaluations. However, if what we want to know is how the public deviates from strict rationality, it is hard to imagine a better basis for comparison. Professional forecasters do exactly what many researchers and political observers argue citizens themselves should do—namely, make systematic and thorough analyses of economic conditions and form opinions based on these assessments.

In order to get a sense of their overall evaluation of the economy, forecasters are provided with estimates of economic growth from previous quarters and asked to predict mean economic growth for the quarter in which the survey is being administered. Thus, they are being asked to evaluate the current state of the economy using information from previous quarters as well as to make forecasts of future quarters. At the same time, the public's view of the economy is assessed regularly by Gallup, CBS, ABC, and the Surveys of Consumers, making it feasible to compare assessments of experts to those of the general public. The comparison between the forecasts of professionals and the

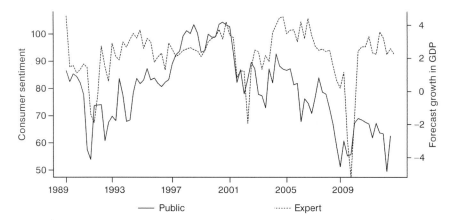

FIGURE 6.1 Consumer sentiment index from Surveys of Consumers, Survey Reasearch Center, University of Michigan (left axis) and forecasted economic growth in GDP from the Survey of Economic Forecasters, 1989–2011 (right axis)

assessments of the public is not without its limitations, since the public is being asked to rate the economy (a very general question) and the forecasters are being asked about a specific aspect of the economy (growth in GDP). Still, economic growth is a broad measure of the state of the economy and thus there is reason to believe that over time the change in these two variables provides a useful comparison between "rational" decision-making and the public.

Both time series are plotted in Figure 6.1 with the right axis representing the scale for the Survey of Professional Forecasters and the left representing the scale for consumer sentiment. The graph does show some clear similarities in the two series as they trend over time and the correlation between them is $\gamma =$ 0.41. Both the public's and the forecasters' evaluations were deeply pessimistic at the time of the recession of 1990–91 and rose after that. The forecasters turned optimistic more quickly than the public, but both evaluations reached a high point during the robust economic conditions of the late 1990s. In the early 2000s, forecasters appeared to be more optimistic than the public, but both trended steadily downward from 2003 until the economy hit rock bottom in 2008 and remained there through 2009. Overall, there are clear similarities in the evaluations made by the public and by economic forecasters, despite the fact that the public is at times inattentive and is consistently subject to partisan influence.

Of course, this similarity is not evidence of rationality if both experts and the public are wildly off base in their assessment of economic conditions. To examine how close to actual conditions these evaluations are, I compare the perceptions of the economy by the public and forecasters to actual economic conditions as measured by real GDP. Table 6.1 reports a regression of experts' and the public's evaluation of the economy on real GDP. In both cases, economic evaluations are significantly related to real economic conditions, but there is a strong similarity in the strength of the relationships. There is a slightly smaller standard error for the residuals of experts (1.38) when compared to the public (1.48); meaning that over the whole time period, the average error for the experts is slightly smaller than that for the public. But this difference does not alter the overall sense that experts do not have an enormous advantage in accurately evaluating overall economic conditions.

Further insight into the similarities and differences between the public and forecasters is evident by looking at the forecast errors of each of the groups described above. If the errors are correlated over time, this suggests that mistakes are repeated and this is inconsistent with most theories of rationality.[1] These forecast errors are obtained from estimating an updating model to obtain period by period forecasts of economic conditions based on each group's assessment of the economy. Formally, this model is:

$$y_t = x_t + \beta_{1t} Econ.Evaluation_{t-1} + v_t$$
$$x_t = x_{t-1} + \omega_{t0}$$
$$\beta_{1t} = \beta_{1t-1} + \omega_{t1}$$

where y_t is real GDP. Thus, the forecast error is $y_t - x_t$ and is calculated iteratively from the model. Looking over the whole time period, the errors of the public and experts show strong similarities.[2] Much of this similarity arises from the fact that many of the big errors (or the turning points if looking at the data in levels) are similar across groups. Big changes in economic conditions occur with some frequency and the public and experts follow a similar pattern in responding to or missing these changes. For example, the biggest error in the series occurred in the third quarter of 2009, when forecasters and the public thought that economic conditions would turn positive (but they in fact remained negative as they had been in the previous four quarters).

These errors can be analyzed in more depth by characterizing the nature of the error structure using ARIMA analysis. If the residuals are "white noise," this indicates that errors do not extend beyond a single time period and that experts or the public do not repeat their errors. On the other hand, when errors are correlated across time periods, there are two ways to characterize their severity. The first is a moving-average (MA) error and this means that an error in one time period tends to lead to an error in the subsequent time period and then disappears. The second error, an autoregressive (AR) error, occurs when errors cascade across many subsequent time periods and this is a more serious violation of rationality. Both types of errors mean that decision-makers do not correct or learn from their mistakes. For the MA errors, the problem lasts a short time; for the AR error, the effect of the error carries on. The analysis of the residuals

TABLE 6.1   Relationship between growth in real GDP and expert and public evaluations of the economy, 1989–2011

Variable	Expert	Public
Constant	0.593★★	–5.05★★★
	(0.244)	(0.94)
Economic evaluation	0.850★★★	0.094★★★
	(0.089)	(0.012)
Observations	91	91
R^2	0.496	0.421
Residual SE	1.38	1.48

Standard errors in parentheses ★★★ p<0.01, ★★ p<0.05, ★ p<0.1

shows that both partisans, the public overall, and forecasters have a moving-average structure to their errors. The moving-average (MA) component, θ, is approximately 0.35 for all the series. In other words, errors in one time period extend to the following time period, but do not continue across all subsequent time periods. This shows that neither the public nor forecasters are perfectly rational and the fact that they make similar types of errors might explain the close correspondence of the two series over time.[3]

For the purposes of this study of citizens and their decision-making process and abilities, this comparison of experts and citizens shows that the ideal of strict rationality is not satisfied by experts, that is people whose job is to calculate their best estimate of the state of the economy make similar (or correlated) errors. There are a variety of reasons that might explain why experts are prone to make errors. First, no matter what model they use to assess the economy, these experts rely on similar information. So if there are errors in the most recent economic data (and macroeconomic data are routinely revised to correct such errors), forecasters are likely to make similar errors based on flaws in the data. Second, forecasters are likely to be risk averse and reluctant to report results that deviate too far from typical forecasts. There are rewards for being better than the other forecasters, but these are small compared to the costs of reporting a forecast that is wildly off base. This means that the experts will tend to underestimate dramatic increases or decreases as they try to keep their estimates in the "normal" range. Third, as a result of their training, these experts hold similar views about how economic factors are related to each other, thus, their modeling strategies are likely to be quite similar.[4]

To explore further the abilities of professional forecasters, I gathered information on the ten forecasters who had participated the most in the Survey of Professional Forecasters from 1985 to 2012.[5] This group of forecasters each participated about 75 times, in other words, they each made about 75 quarterly forecasts. However, there were only 50 forecasts in which all ten forecasters participated. From these cases, the individual-level forecast errors were calculated over time by comparing each forecaster's prediction about GDP in the quarter of the survey to the actual estimate of GDP that was reported after the survey was conducted. In other words, for the first quarter of 1990, I would compare a forecaster's predicted GDP to the actual estimate of GDP for the first quarter of 1990 released later that year. A comparison was made over time by correlating all ten forecasters' errors in the 50 overlapping cases. The quarterly forecast errors showed a remarkable correlation with an average correlation across the ten forecasters of about 0.80. The most accurate forecaster had a correlation of 0.41 with the worst forecaster, indicating that the best and the worst are not that far apart in their forecasts. And the best forecaster's errors were correlated at 0.80 with several of the other forecasters, meaning that the best forecaster was not especially different from most of the others. Overall, the analysis shows a remarkably high level of correlated errors. The explanations for this level of agreement are hard to pin down precisely but include the previously mentioned factors 1) not wanting to deviate too far from what is likely to be the consensus forecast or 2) similar tools and methods leading to similar errors.

Having established the similarity between experts' assessments of the economy and the public as a whole, the remaining question is whether partisans are worse than experts. To address this question, partisan evaluations (as described in previous chapters) are regressed on real GDP. These are reported in Table 6.2.[6] There are some differences in the strength of the relationship among the partisan groups. The standard errors of the residuals are larger for Democrats (1.54) and Republicans (1.62) than the public as a whole (1.48), as reported in Table 6.1. Thus, the average evaluation of the two parties as captured in the public's overall evaluation is somewhat closer to experts' evaluations than each of the partisan groups alone.[7] This is an important finding since it suggests that partisan differences are overcome at the aggregate level partly through the process of averaging the "signals" provided by those loyal to the Democratic and Republican parties.

The rise of political polarization in contemporary politics has led political analysts and observers to wonder about its corrosive effects on public opinion (Mann & Ornstein 2012). A comparison of the errors made by experts and the public prior to the heightened partisanship of the current era can, to some extent, illuminate the impact of partisanship on public opinion. Since the context for making economic evaluations shifts over time because of recessions, economic expansions, financial crises, etc, the expert evaluations can serve as a kind of control for citizen evaluations—that is, if citizens perform worse than experts

TABLE 6.2 Relationship between growth in real GDP and expert and partisan evaluations of the economy, 1989–2011

Variable	Democrat	Republican	Independent
Constant	–3.589★★★	–3.73★★★	–4.926★★★
	(0.853)	(0.996)	(0.947)
Economic evaluation	2.561★★★	2.32★★★	3.00★★★
	(0.354)	(0.369)	(0.380)
Observations	91	91	91
R^2	0.365	0.306	0.407
Residual SE	1.54	1.622	1.496

Standard errors in parentheses ★★★ p<0.01, ★★ p<0.05, ★ p<0.1

in a partisan era, there is some evidence that partisanship is making overall assessments worse, controlling for different contexts. Using the Lewinsky scandal in 1998 as a benchmark for heightened polarization, the size of the errors for citizens relative to those of experts is expanding. I calculated the root mean squared error (RMSE) as a measure of the average difference between the public and experts across time and compare its size before and after the scandal. For the period from 1989 to 1998 (before the Lewinsky scandal), the RMSE is 1.53, whereas after the scandal (1998 to 2011), the RMSE is slightly bigger 1.73. Thus, there does appear to be some evidence that partisanship leads to less accurate assessments of economic conditions, but the effects do not appear to be large.

For the purposes of the analysis conducted here, these limitations show the difficulty of establishing ideal conditions for rational decision-making, either by experts or citizens. The upshot is that the ideal standard of strict rationality is likely to be too high a bar for assessing citizens' rationality. However, despite the imperfect nature of collective rationality, the public's assessment of the state of the economy is not too far afield from that of experts. This similarity might arise either because the experts aren't as good as we think they are (see above) or both experts and citizens capture the major turning points leading to a convergence of views. A third possibility is that through "byproduct learning" the public gains as much useful information as experts for making overall assessments of the economy (Prior 2007, Haller & Norpoth 1997).[8] In the end, it does appear that, despite individual-level errors, the public's reliance on information short cuts (like party cues) and selective use of information in making judgments allow it to act more rationally than might be expected, if we use a comparison to experts as a standard of rationality.[9]

Conclusion

A fundamental tenet of modern democracy is that collective public opinion is meaningful and coherent—otherwise why should we consider it a key factor in making political decisions? Defending public opinion can be difficult, however. Those who study politics at the individual level continue to find evidence that citizens do not know key facts that are essential to making sound judgments. The most convincing defense of the coherence of public opinion is provided by Page and Shapiro (1992) in *The Rational Public*. They argue that through the "miracle of aggregation" collective public opinion becomes stable and meaningful because enough individuals are attentive to political news and events to cancel out the inattention and misjudgments of the uninformed. But in their defense of the miracle of aggregation, they fail to account for the role of key features of modern politics: partisanship, the selective use of information, and the shifting salience of issues. I argue that these specifically political factors are crucial for explaining public opinion, but they do not undercut its rationality.

As the analysis here shows, the signal—the meaningful message—in public opinion is evident despite some "errors" or noise clouding the message. I demonstrated in Chapter 2 that in time series of some common polling questions, public opinion does, in fact, constitute more signal than noise. But in an important twist, partisanship—rather than making people myopic—seems to be the primary source of the signal. In other words, the analysis demonstrates that collective public opinion is informed about essential news and events and that partisanship organizes this information.

By analyzing in Chapter 3 some original datasets that separate out the opinions of Democrats and Republicans regarding presidential performance and economic conditions, I demonstrated the different dynamics of public opinion for partisan groups. The analysis focuses on the dynamics of the in-party (the party aligned with the president) and the out-party (the party opposing the president) and how they evolve in different ways. In a finding consistent with micro-level explanations of how individuals make decisions, those supportive of the incumbent president tend to ignore negative news about presidential performance and economic conditions and seek out news that things are going well. At the same time, those who do not share the same party as the incumbent president (the out-party) tend to seek out negative information and pay less attention to good news. This analysis shows that partisans shift their information seeking depending on their support for the president and this plays a key role in the evolution of collective opinion.

The information-processing model described in Chapter 4 builds upon the idea that different segments of the public (particularly partisans) sometimes accept and sometimes resist new information. Applying the model to partisan opinion shows the important role that prior information plays in how partisans update. Partisan groups (and the public as a whole) do not evaluate their preferences anew as issues make their way onto and off the political agenda. Instead, the prior assessments of issues are used to filter new information and to update opinions in light of the strength of this information. In this updating model, not all information carries the same weight and this is a more realistic approach to model the way that partisans and the public use information to formulate new opinions.

The analysis of collective opinion in the book through Chapter 4 stressed the importance of partisan groups and their contribution to the "signal" in public opinion. However, it is important to understand opinion as a whole, combining the effects of the partisan groups. As seen in Chapter 5, overall public opinion is characterized by regime shifts, that is a fundamental shift in the way that the public uses information. Some of this is due to partisanship, particularly in more recent periods, but these regime shifts have occurred with some frequency prior to the current partisan era. This change in the use of information can be thought of as a new updating model, one in which the weight attached to information changes in light of emerging conditions. Shifting the updating model over time, is also evidence of a type of learning and the fit between the data and changepoint models suggest that this learning occurs in spurts rather than continuously. The public seems to rely on one model for a time and then circumstances change, and the model is reset and relied on for a while until conditions require another change.

Arguments for the "rationality" of collective opinion must inevitably confront the disconnect between micro-level, individual-level studies and macro-arguments for the benefits of aggregation. The micro-level argument details the shortcomings of individuals, whether they arise from myopia, limited attention, lack of knowledge, or weak ideological foundations. Despite the fact that the sources of the errors are many, the resolution of these problems share a common foundation, one segment of the population is the source of noise and the other is the source of signal. The attentive versus inattentive public is one characterization of this problem. Erikson, MacKuen, and Stimson (2002) emphasize this conceptualization in their argument of the meaningfulness of aggregate opinion. They do suggest that there can be some "fuzziness" about the nature of the groups and their consistency across issues, but nonetheless, in the end, part of the public tracks information in the political and economic environment and adjusts its opinion upward or downward in light of positive or negative news and provides the consistency between opinion and information. Page and Shapiro (1992) do not use the language of an attentive and inattentive public in their defense of the "rational public" but they stress that the "miracle of aggregation" leads to coherent collective opinion as errors cancel out, leaving a signal that is coherent, in the sense that it moves up and down in concert with changes in the environment.

In this book, I argue, along with Page and Shapiro, that aggregation does provide a relatively coherent signal, but contend that the signal is principally the byproduct of partisan updating rather than a core set of knowledgeable individuals. As noted by Shapiro and Bloch-Elkon (2008), if partisanship serves as the foundation for the signal in aggregate opinion, a new information-processing model is required, one that moves beyond the stimulus–response model upon which most analyses of aggregate opinion are constructed. With its reliance on priors, the Bayesian updating model constitutes an important development beyond the stimulus–response model and makes it feasible to incorporate the effects of partisanship as well as shifting attention and context into the analysis of aggregate opinion. The key change introduced by a Bayesian updating model is that the public processes information through its prior assessments, rather than simply responding to or ignoring new information. In addition to providing a more complete and politically grounded model for how the public processes information, the Bayesian updating model implies that the public also learns over time. The shifting regimes and the associated change in the weight that is attached to information mean that the public is changing the way that it processes information over time, and this type of learning can be thought of as a form of rationality.

Updating Models

The updating model here bears some similarity to models of aggregate behavior developed by economists, and a comparison of them provides useful perspective on the key attributes of a more realistic model of aggregate behavior. Of particular interest is work by economists who have tried to study aggregate behavior by weakening some of the standard assumptions in information processing, namely that rational decision-makers will use all available information when updating. Mankiw and Reis (2006), Reis (2006), and Sims (2006), for example, recognize that complete information processing is not particularly realistic or perhaps even desirable. At the heart of this reformulation is the idea that information is costly to obtain, or put another way, it takes a lot of work to be fully informed. When accounting for information costs, what counts as rational looks different. Reis (2006) and Sims (2006) propose models of "rational" inattention as a way to understand aggregate behavior. In their view, information is "sticky" and only periodically updated. In the context of economic evaluations, this means that the public doesn't constantly scour news reports for changes in the economy; instead, people rely on news to come to them and perhaps only to periodically seek out new information. To put it more concretely, if the economy is in a recession, most people are unlikely to notice a slight fall in the unemployment rate, say from 8.5 percent to 8.1 percent. If unemployment is high, the details are not particularly important. When information signals a change away from a high level, updating will occur.

This periodic updating process is also consistent with the idea of regime shifts developed as part of the Bayesian updating model. Rather than smooth transitions in the weight that is attached to information, periodic attention should lead the public to periodically rethink its assessment of the economy and to settle into a new regime until news or events force people to refocus and perhaps to reassess.

Finally, a related idea is that aggregate behavior is influenced by habits (Reis 2006). In other words, people develop rules of thumb or heuristics for processing information. Thus, each new piece of information is not treated in the abstract but weighed in light of previous decisions about the significance of new information. Obviously, in the context of politics, parties help establish habits, allowing people to make sense of the avalanche of information broadcast via television, the radio, print media, the internet, and social media. As shown in Chapter 4, it is useful to think about these habits (or party cues) as priors, or as past judgments that play some role in how current information is used.

Party

Given the contentiousness of modern American politics and the role that partisan animosity played in this development, some final reflections on the role of partisanship are in order. The corrosive impact of partisanship on the conduct of politics in Washington, DC and statehouses around the country are evident in daily news reports. The causes of the polarization in Washington are well documented in Mann and Ornstein (2012) and the unfortunate effect of this is that enduring problems, like an aging infrastructure and immigration, remain unaddressed. The consequences of this polarization on public opinion is more difficult to pin down and an ongoing topic of research (Fiorina 2006, Levendusky 2009).

For purposes of this study, the question is to what extent does partisanship undermine or improve the quality of public opinion. It is easy to find anecdotal survey results that point to the ways in which partisan loyalties lead to partisan bias. For example, two similarly worded questions were used in 2006 and 2013 to assess Americans' attitudes about the National Security Administration's (NSA) surveillance program. In both surveys, a slight majority of Americans indicated that they supported the surveillance program as a means to combat terrorism, with 51 percent responding that the program was acceptable in 2006 and 56 percent in 2013. However, when looking at the partisan breakdown of support, the surveys show that 75 percent of Republicans thought that spying was acceptable in 2006, when George W. Bush was president, and this support fell to 52 percent in 2013 under the Obama administration. This pattern is reversed when looking at support among Democrats. In 2006, 37 percent found the NSA surveillance program acceptable, but in 2013, when Barack Obama was president, 64 percent said that the spying program was acceptable.[10] This anecdotal evidence finds some support in experimental studies that show the impact of partisan cues on opinion in a variety of settings, from war deaths to energy policy. In addition, in their recent study of partisanship, Lavine, Johnston, and Steenbergen (2012) find that those who are the weakest partisans (what they call "ambivalent" partisans) are the most likely to update their opinions in light of new evidence and be least susceptible to manipulation by party elites.

The analysis reported here, however, paints a different picture of the role of partisanship. Chapter 2 demonstrates that partisanship helps low-information people, in particular, to make fewer errors when judging the state of the economy or the performance of the president. In addition, when looking over time, the signal in public opinion comes from those who are partisans rather than those who are best informed. The movement in public opinion is often the byproduct of partisan differences diminishing during times of crisis and repeated news about economic performance, either positive or negative.

For example, Republicans responded to consistent news about the economic expansion under President Clinton by positively assessing the economy. And in early 2008, with the news of worsening economic conditions and a bursting of the housing bubble, they began to view the economy negatively, before the financial crisis fully developed in October of that year. Finally, the comparison of public, partisan, and expert opinion described in this chapter shows that the public as a whole satisfies at least one criterion for judging its rationality: similarity to judgments of experts. As described above, professional forecasters are not perfectly rational; they formulate their forecasts and assess the economy in ways that are consistent with our conceptualization of a "rational actor." Although there are differences between the judgments of experts and the public, these differences appear to be relatively small.

The question then is how to reconcile these findings from individual-level studies that claim partisanship is detrimental to the quality of public opinion with the analysis presented here showing that it is helpful and essential. First, it is important to recognize that there are empirical as well as normative counterarguments to the claim that intense partisanship is detrimental to the quality of public opinion. Those researching the impact of partisanship on public opinion argue that strong partisan cues often do what they are supposed to do—indeed what is required of them in the responsible parties framework— provide clear signals to ordinary citizens about what position they should take on the broad scope of issues that make their way onto the political agenda. Bolsen, Druckman, and Cook (2014, 253) argue that "relying on one's partisanship" (e.g., a partisan directional goal) in the face of limited policy information is "smarter" than trying to assess the policy's content oneself. Even in the face of the intense partisanship of contemporary politics, Levendusky (2009, 138) makes the case that partisan sorting may be a good thing since parties are "the thread that connects the mass public to government policies." In addition, according to Lau and Redlawsk (2006), partisanship helps people to vote "correctly" (i.e., in a way that is consistent with their preferences).

Political theorists Russell Muirhead (2014) and Nancy Rosenblum (2008) lend support to the argument for the necessity and usefulness of partisanship in modern democratic governance. Muirhead contends that parties are woven into the fabric of modern democracies. They are needed to make sense of complex issues, guide voters in low-information contests, get voters motivated to participate, and organize legislatures (both state and national). He argues that the negative view of parties arises from an overly idealized conception of good citizenship in which "citizens should be impartial, like judges, and objective, like scientists" (Muirhead 2014, 9). From this perspective, partisanship seems like a crutch, providing cues and shortcuts that are "substitutes for paying attention to politics" (Muirhead 2014, 9). As Muirhead and others argue, if party is necessary at the time of elections, it isn't reasonable to expect their effects to disappear from public discussion and public opinion in between elections. Thus, in contemporary politics, we do not necessarily like it when partisanship produces feuding and intransigence, but there is a recognition that we need parties.

Rosenblum (2008) provides a spirited defense of partisanship. She argues that partisan citizens are to be celebrated—they are engaged in the political process and help to make needed decisions. Parties themselves, she contends, are a vital part of democracy, structuring political debates, defining the "battle lines" on an issue that are necessary to make choices, and "creat[ing], not just reflect[ing], political interests and opinions" (Rosenblum 2008, 7). Importantly, she makes the case that true "Independents," who are often viewed as the ideal, dispassionate citizens, are often the least informed about politics and contribute far less to the democratic process than partisans.

The analysis presented here is consistent with this idea that partisans are an essential part of the political process, shaping the dynamics and structure of collective public opinion and that this is not to be regretted. As shown here, partisanship contributes to meaningful collective public opinion and that is essential to the functioning of modern democratic systems. Surely, there are dangers associated with extreme partisanship like a *refusal* as opposed to a *reluctance* to update in light of new information; but when studying assessments of economic conditions and presidential performance, partisans do appear to eventually update their views in light of information even if they do not like the news. Indeed, there is some evidence that even on the issue of climate change, Republicans are moving closer to Democrats in their belief that human activity has an impact on the earth's temperature.

In fact, I turn here at the end to issue to show how the key components of collective opinion (e.g., partisanship, regime change) and the Bayesian updating model generalize to other settings. The general perception is that climate change is one of the defining issues of this polarized era, with Democrats and Republicans sharply divided on the seriousness and immediacy of climate change. As such, one might be tempted to think that opinion on the issue is static, with little movement by either party. However, a 2013 report from Pew Research Center shows something quite different. Respondents were asked the following question in nine separate polls from 2006 to 2013: "From what you've read and heard, is there solid evidence that the average temperature on earth has been getting warmer over the past few decades, or not?" Surprisingly, the highest level of support for each of the parties occurred in 2006 with 90 percent of Democrats, 79 percent of Independents, and 59 percent of Republicans believing that there is solid evidence of the earth warming. After 2006, support for the position that the earth is warming steadily fell for each of the groups from 2006 to 2009. In 2009, support for the solid evidence position was 75 percent for Democrats, 53 percent for Independents, and 35 percent for Republicans. Thus, support for the position that climate change is real fell 24 percentage points for Republicans. Support among Democrats fell a more modest 14 percentage points. Since we know that the problem of climate change didn't get better during this time period, it seems likely that people's attention was diverted to economic issues, e.g., the bursting of the housing bubble followed by the recession of 2008. This suggests that collective opinion experienced a "regime shift" in which economic conditions altered people's assessment of climate change. This is consistent with the updating model described here in which collective opinion undergoes fundamental restructuring, and the change does not support the idea that the public systematically assesses new information in the same way over time, as implied in a stimulus–response model of updating.

After 2009, attitudes about climate change reversed course. Each of the partisan groups showed a steady rise in concern about climate change from 2009 to 2013, but the trend for each was markedly different. Among Democrats, support for the position that "climate change is having an impact now" rose from 75 percent to 88 percent and this was the smallest for any of the partisan groups. Surprisingly, for Republicans, the rise in support was higher with 35 percent believing that there was "solid evidence of climate change now" in 2009 to 50 percent supporting this idea in 2013. Part of the explanation is likely due to the fact that from 2009 to 2013, there were a number of heavily reported record-breaking weather events, like Hurricane Sandy, that led all partisan groups to support the idea that climate change is at work right now. However, the rate at which the partisan groups updated varied. Democrats had a slow steady rise from 2009 forward, while Independents and Republicans had a steeper increase in their support for the immediacy of climate change. The fact that all groups updated is important, since it shows that even though Republicans have strong "priors" that lead them to be skeptical of climate change, they did in fact update in response to news reports and mounting evidence of climate change (like the record snowfall in Washington, DC, in the winter of 2009–2010). But the impact of this news varied across the partisan groups. Democrats, already overwhelmingly supportive of the idea of climate change, showed the smallest change, while Republicans and Independents experienced more dramatic updating. The public as a whole moved from 57 percent agreeing that there was solid evidence of climate change in 2009 to 67 percent in 2013. As noted in the analysis of economic conditions, presidential approval and related events, much of the movement in aggregate opinion is the byproduct of one party moving toward the other. In the case of climate change, the movement in the overall series from 2009 to 2013 is primarily due to changes in the attitudes of Republicans, reinforcing the idea that partisanship is an essential contributor to the dynamics of collective opinion.

Rationality

Arguing for any kind of political rationality at the turn of the twenty-first century may seem either heroic or foolish. With daily reports of party politics stymying any attempts at collective problem-solving in the areas of economic, health, or environmental policy and deep divisions within the public regarding a range of social issues (race, abortion), order and meaning are difficult to come by. A central component of this discord is partisanship. Just as at the time of the American founding, the role of parties (and factions) is seen as antagonistic to good politics. As Rosenblum (2008, 16) writes, in modern times "we recognize 'partisan' as invective."

But, despite the obvious problems traced to partisanship (Republicans are much more likely than Democrats to think that Obama was not born in the US; Democrats thought that economic outcomes were worse after Ronald Reagan left office than before [Bartels 2002]), researchers argue that it is a necessary feature of modern democracies from both a normative and empirical perspective. In her assessment of partisanship, Rosenblum argues that it is illusory and misguided to think that people will approach politics from a neutral, rational standpoint and make judgments based on the weight of the evidence. Inevitably, citizens must bring a perspective to political decision-making and this perspective is beneficial since it focuses their search for information, facilitates political coalitions, etc.

Studies of political decision-making point to the essential role that parties play in citizens' information processing. Research on decision-making in nearly all settings highlights the need for individuals to simplify the decision-making environment, by limiting the number of choices, using heuristics, cueing off others, or habit. The setting for modern politics is complex, with a constant swirl of issues and related news, and the only reasonable way to proceed is to rely on heuristics and information shortcuts (Lavine, Johnston & Steenbergen 2012). A unique feature of modern politics is that it is highly structured around parties (Aldrich 1995), and this will continue to influence public opinion. For much of the modern era, the partisan structure of institutions has shaped the vote choice and legislative activities in Congress. The news reporting itself can contribute to the partisan divide by constructing two sides to every issue and typically recruiting a Democrat to present one side and a Republican the other. In addition, the cable news reinforces partisan divisions by providing news with a perspective (e.g., MSNBC and Fox News), and this has led to a greater reliance by the public on self-selected media (Prior 2007).[1]

Recognizing that the public as a whole relies on an updating process that falls short of the idealized, rational decision-maker does not mean giving up on political rationality entirely. First, as shown here, this idealized decision-maker is more illusory than real. Second, even with an updating process that is heavily influenced by political realities (i.e., citizens need partisanship to make sense of the political environment, the flow of news shifts their attention to key issues and helps them make choices that are consistent with their goals and values), evaluations of the economy match those of experts to a remarkable degree. This does not mean that partisanship is always helpful. It does appear that the public's evaluations of the economy are somewhat more off-track in the highly partisan environment of twenty-first-century politics. But, as this analysis of opinion over time shows, the politics of today is not necessarily the politics of tomorrow—contexts shift, issues rise and fall, politicians come and go—but, importantly, the public adapts to and learns from these changes and collective opinion maintains a high degree of coherence and legitimacy.

Notes

1. This view of errors derives from theories of rational expectations and they are summarized in Krause (2000).
2. A figure that plots the errors for each group over time is available in the online supplement at http://gemcavoy.wp.uncg.edu/cpr/.
3. If the public's errors had an AR structure and experts had an MA error, the evaluations of the public and experts would have quite different dynamics over time.
4. This paragraph draws on the discussions of forecasters in Taleb (2001) and Taleb (2006).
5. The individual-level forecasts are available from the Real-Time Research Data Center of the Federal Reserve Bank of Philadelphia (http://www.philadelphiafed. org/research-and-data/real-time-center/survey-of-professional-forecasters/, accessed March 12, 2013).
6. The errors are shown in a figure in the online supplement at http://gemcavoy. wp.uncg.edu/cpr/.
7. These findings are consistent with those of Enns, Kellstedt, and McAvoy (2012) and Enns and McAvoy (2012), who describe these partisan differences in more detail.
8. These researchers use "byproduct learning" to describe the way that ordinary citizens pick up information in the environment to make informed decisions, but without making a conscious effort to acquire relevant information. They accumulate this information as a byproduct of talking to other people and living in an information rich environment.

9. Mankiw, Reis, and Wolfers (2004) and Carroll (2003) find the same level of convergence between the views of experts and citizens in their studies of inflation expectations.
10. These survey results were reported in Pew Research Center (2013). The 2006 data came from a ABC News/*Washington Post* survey and the results for 2013 came from a Pew Research Center/*Washington Post* poll.
11. As Aldrich (1995, 8) notes, it is difficult to find an issue of interest to pollsters that is not divided along partisan lines. The extent to which the ordinary citizens pay attention to one-sided news is an active area of research with some arguing that only the most attentive and partisan viewers watching Fox News and MSNBC (Ladd 2012).

Bibliography

Aldrich, John H. 1995. *Why Parties? The Origin and Transformation of Political Parties in America.* Chicago, IL: The University of Chicago Press.

Bartels, Larry. 2002. "Beyond the Running Tally: Partisan Bias in Political Perceptions." *Political Behavior* 24(2):117–150.

Bolsen, Toby, James N. Druckman & Fay Lomax Cook. 2014. "The Influence of Partisan Motivated Reasoning on Public Opinion." *Political Behavior* 36(2):235–262.

Carroll, Christopher D. 2003. "Macroeconomic Expectations of Households and Professional Forecasters." *Quarterly Journal of Economics* 118(1):269–298.

Enns, Peter. K. & Gregory E. McAvoy. 2012. "The Role of Partisanship in Aggregate Opinion." *Political Behavior* 34(4):627–651.

Enns, Peter K., Paul M. Kellstedt & Gregory E. McAvoy. 2012. "The Consequences of Partisanship in Economic Perceptions." *Public Opinion Quarterly* 76(2):287–310.

Erikson, Robert S., Michael B. MacKuen & James A. Stimson. 2002. *The Macro Polity.* New York: Cambridge University Press.

Fiorina, Morris. 2006. *Culture War?: The Myth Of A Polarized America.* New York: Pearson Longman.

Haller, H. Brandon & Helmut Norpoth. 1997. "Reality Bites: News Exposure and Economic Opinion." *Public Opinion Quarterly* 61(4):555–575.

Krause, George A. 2000. "Testing for the Strong Form of Rational Expectations with Heterogeneously Informed Agents." *Political Analysis* 8:285–305.

Ladd, Jonathan M. 2012. *Why Americans Hate the Media and How It Matters.* Princeton, NJ: Princeton University Press.

Lau, Richard R. & David P. Redlawsk. 2006. *How Voters Decide: Information Processing during Election Campaigns.* Cambridge: Cambridge University Press.

Lavine, Howard G., Christopher D. Johnston & Marco R. Steenbergen. 2012. *The Ambivalent Partisan: How Critical Loyalty Promotes Democracy.* Oxford: Oxford University Press.

Levendusky, Matthew. 2009. *The Partisan Sort.* Chicago, IL: University of Chicago Press.

Mankiw, N. Gregory. & Ricardo Reis. 2006. "Pervasive Stickiness." *American Economic Review* 96(2):164–169.

Mankiw, N. Gregory, Ricardo Reis & Justin Wolfers. 2004. "Disagreement about Inflation Expectations." In M. Gertler and K. Rogoff (eds) *NBER Macroeconomics Annual 18,* pp. 209–270. Cambridge, MA: NBER.

Mann, T.E. & N.J. Ornstein. 2012. *It's Even Worse Than It Looks: How the American Constitutional System Collided with the New Politics of Extremism.* New York: Basic Books.

McCarty, Nolan, Keith T. Poole & Howard Rosenthal. 2006. *Polarized America: The Dance of Ideology and Unequal Riches.* Cambridge, MA: MIT Press.

Muirhead, Russell. 2014. *The Promise of Party in a Polarized Age.* Cambridge, MA: Harvard University Press.

Page, Benjamin I. & Robert Y. Shapiro. 1992. *The Rational Public: Fifty Years of Trends in Americans' Policy Preferences.* Chicago, IL: University of Chicago Press.

Pew Research Center. 2013. "Majority Views NSA Phone Tracking as Acceptable Anti-terror Tactic." http://www.people-press.org/2013/06/10/majority-views-nsa-phone-tracking-as-acceptable-anti-terror-tactic/, -*accessed October 14, 2014.*

Prior, Markus. 2007. *Post-Broadcast Democracy.* Cambridge: Cambridge University Press.

Reis, Ricardo. 2006. "Inattentive Consumers." *Journal of Monetary Economics* 53(8) 1761–1800.

Rosenblum, Nancy L. 2008. *On the Side of the Angels: An Appreciation of Parties and Partisanship.* Princeton, NJ: Princeton University Press.

Shapiro, Robert Y. & Yaeli Bloch-Elkon. 2008. "Do The Facts Speak For Themselves? Partisan Disagreement As A Challenge To Democratic Competence." *Critical Review* 20(1):115–139.

Sims, Christopher. A. 2006. "Rational Inattention: Beyond the Linear-Quadratic Case." *American Economic Review* 96(2):158–163.

Taleb, Nassim Nicholas. 2001. *Fooled by Randomness.* New York: Random House.

Taleb, Nassim Nicholas. 2006. *The Black Swan: The Impact of the Highly Improbable.* New York: Random House

INDEX

9/11 30, 53, 59, 73, 99

ABC News, *see* polls
Affordable Care Act (ACA) 1–3, 13
Afghanistan 7
aggregate opinion 3–4, 6, 8–10, 12–14,
    16, 23–4, 28, 34–6, 42, 49–50, 52–3,
    60, 63–4, 69–70, 74, 77, 80, 88, 92,
    95, 102, 109, 113, 121–2, 127
Albert, J. 90
Aldrich, J. 127
Alesina, A. et al. 102
Al-Qaeda 5, 22
Althaus, S. 5, 28, 39
Alvarez, M. 43
ambivalence 43
ambivalent partisans 11
American International Group (AIG)
    44
attentive public 4–6, 23, 33–4, 39, 42,
    64, 92, 109
autoregressive integrated moving
    average (ARIMA) models 58, 66,
    116
autoregressive models 116, 128

Bartels, L. 5, 9–10, 35, 39, 48, 127
Bayesian analysis 70, 73–4, 77
Bayesian updating 6–8, 16–17, 43, 64,
    69–71, 73, 76–7, 80, 87, 89, 110, 113,
    122–3, 125

Bayes' Theorem 70–1, 73, 90
Beck, N. 9, 110
benchmarking 6, 13, 114, 119
Bendor, J. 94
Binder, S. 15
Bloch-Elkon, Y. 122
Bolsen, 12, 124
Bond, J. et al. 110
bounded rationality 16–17, 94
Brehm, J. 43
Brodie, M. et al. 44
Brody, R. 58
Bullock, J. 8, 63, 71, 76–7, 90
Bush, G. H. W. 31–2, 59, 65, 105
Bush, G. W. 7, 26, 31–3, 51–6, 59, 61,
    64–6, 90, 99, 107, 123
byproduct theory 35

Campbell, A. et al. 4, 9, 15
Carmines, E. and Stimson, J. 31
Carroll, C. 114
Carsey, T. 12
Carter, J. 59, 65–6
casualties 49, 110
CBS, *see* polls
changepoint models 94–5, 97–102,
    105–6, 108–9, 121
Chib, S. 97
climate change 41–2, 125–7
Clinton, B. 11, 26, 32, 51, 59, 61, 63,
    65–6, 83, 85, 100, 105, 124

collective opinion 3–5, 9–10, 16–17, 23, 34, 95, 114, 120–1, 125–8
conditional variance 78, 80–1, 90
confirmation bias 50, 78
consumer sentiment 32–3, 56, 83–4, 86, 115
Cornhusker Kickback 1

death panels 1–3, 13
De Boef, S. and Kellstedt P. 44, 90
Dimock, M. 41
Druckman, J. 3, 5, 10, 12, 14, 33, 93, 102–3, 107, 124
Duch, R. M. et al. 11

Ebola 14
economic evaluations 15, 32–3, 38, 41, 50–1, 53, 57, 66, 70, 79–80, 82, 86–8, 90, 93, 95–102, 104, 109–10, 114, 116, 118, 122
economic expansion 51, 99–100, 124
economic forecasters 17, 114–19, 124, 128
economists 114, 122
education: impact on public opinion 15, 34–8, 41–2, 61–3; example of updating 71–4
Edwards, G. 103
Enns, P. 10, 15, 51, 60, 66, 82, 128
Erikson, R. et al. 4–5, 7, 9–10, 23, 34, 48–9, 53, 60, 90, 121
Evans, G. 10
experimental studies 10, 17, 39, 48–50, 78, 124

favorable economic news 83–4
Feldman, S. and Zaller, J. 43
financial crisis 8, 52, 55, 79–80, 83, 88, 100, 124
Fiorina, M. 123

Gaines, B. 6, 11, 48–50, 69
Gallup, see polls
Gelman, A. 70, 98
General Social Survey (GSS) 60–1
Gerber, A. 44, 49, 53, 73
Gingrich, N. 74–5
Goss, K. 93
Green, D. et al. 73
Greider, D. 103
Grenada, invasion of 11
Gronke, P. 59
Gulf War 30, 59, 110

habits 16, 92, 95, 97, 102, 109, 123
Haller, H. and Norpoth, H. 32, 119
health care 1–3
Holian, D. 61
honeymoons 11
Hurricane Katrina 94
Hurricane Sandy 126
Hussein, S. 5, 99

inattention 9, 44, 120, 122
inattentive public 4, 6, 16, 23, 34, 39, 92, 121
individual-level analysis 2, 4–5, 8–10, 12, 16, 23, 33, 48, 50, 70, 113, 118–19, 121, 124, 128
information processing 2, 6, 8, 10, 49, 69–83, 85–90, 92, 94–5, 114, 122, 127
in-party 10, 52, 55–9, 64, 79–82, 90, 109, 120
Iranian hostage crisis 59, 99
Iraq 5, 7, 11, 22, 49, 54, 110
issue salience 3–4, 11, 61, 109, 113–14, 120

Jackman, S. 29, 70–1
Jacobs, L. 1, 61, 93
Jacobson, G. 53, 107
Johnson, L. 55, 65–6

Kaiser Tracking Poll, see polls
Kalman filter 24, 29, 43–4, 73, 75–6, 78, 80–1, 88
Kalman gain 43, 74–8, 80–2, 88–90, 107, 109
Kellstedt, P. 51, 60, 66, 82, 90, 128
Kennedy, J. 53, 64–5
Kernell, S. 93
Kim, C. and Nelson, C. 89
Kim, S. et al. 8, 77
Krause, G. and Granato, J. 34, 128
Krosnick, J. 93
Kull, S. et al. 9
Kuwait, invasion of 99

Ladd, J. 93
Lapidos, J. 41
Lau, R. and Redlawsk, D. 16, 39, 125
Lavine, H. et al. 11, 124, 127
Layman, G. 12
LearnBayes, see R packages
Lebo, M. and Cassino, D. 15, 49

Lehman Brothers 44, 114
Levendusky, M. 12, 15, 107, 123–4
Lewinsky, M. 119
Lindblom, C. 94
Lippmann, W. 4–5, 15
Lupia, A. et al. 16

macro politics 5–6, 33, 49, 94, 103, 121
Mankiw, G. 114, 122
Mann, T. and Ornstein, N. 118, 123
MCMC 95–6, 101, 105, 108, 110
MCMCpack, see R packages
Michigan Surveys of Consumers, see polls
micro-level analysis 5, 9, 10, 13, 49, 94, 120–1
miracle of aggregation 5, 10, 16, 36, 42, 64, 113, 120–1
Monogan, J. 66
motivated reasoning 3, 5, 10, 16, 49–50, 55–8, 64, 69–70, 77, 79–82
Mueller, J. 59
Muirhead, R. 125

National Security Administration (NSA) 123
Nelson, B. 1
Newman, B. and A. Forcehimes 59–60, 105
news reception 83–6, 88
Nixon, R. 55, 59, 65–6
Noriega, M. 59

Obama, B. 7, 25–7, 51–4, 56, 59, 64–6, 107, 123–4, 127; misperceived as Muslim 22
Oklahoma bombing 73
out-party 10 50, 52, 55–9, 79–82, 90, 120

Page, B. I. and Shapiro, R. Y. 4, 7, 10, 16, 23, 33, 35, 42, 44, 120–2
partisan bias 10–11, 17, 39, 48, 50, 61, 102, 109, 123
partisan evaluations 51–3, 63, 66, 118–19
Paul, R. 74–5
Petris, G. and Petrone, S. 26, 73, 90
Pew Research Center, see polls
Pickup, M. 10
polarization 12, 49, 61, 63, 107, 118–19, 123

policy preferences: education, crime, and the environment 60–1, 63
political knowledge 13, 34, 39–40, 78
polls: ABC 15, 34–6, 51, 66, 114; CBS 15, 28–31, 34–6, 44, 51, 66, 114; Gallup 3, 13–15, 25, 28–31, 34–6, 44, 51, 53–6, 66, 74–5, 114; Kaiser Tracking Poll 1, 44; Michigan Surveys of Consumers 26, 32, 50, 85, 98, 115; Pew Research Center 2–3, 41, 126
presidential approval 10–11, 14, 33, 35, 40–1, 44, 53, 56–60, 64–5, 70, 79, 81–3, 93, 102, 104–10, 127
primaries 25–7, 74
priming 93, 103, 109
priors, in public opinion 7, 49–50, 63–4, 69–81, 88, 90, 92, 94, 109–10, 122–3, 126
public opinion: Democrats 1–3, 7, 9–10, 13, 15, 25, 27, 36–7, 41, 48–55, 59, 61–4, 66, 118, 120, 123, 125–7; disaggregated 15, 36–7, 42, 50, 57, 88; economic approval 29–30; foreign policy 14, 28–31, 33, 42, 61, 93, 97, 107; Independents 3, 37, 48, 51, 53, 55, 62, 66, 125–7; management of the economy 26–7; Republicans 2–3, 7, 9–11, 13, 36, 41–2, 48–55, 61–3, 66, 118, 120, 123–7

rally events 59–60, 63
random error 9, 13, 25–6, 28–30, 33, 42–4, 89
rationality 4–5, 8–9, 14–17, 22–3, 33–4, 42, 44, 64, 69, 73, 92, 94, 113–17, 119–22, 124, 127–8
rational public 4–5, 7, 43, 120–1
Reagan, R. 11, 32, 60, 64–5, 127
regimes 6, 8, 11–12, 80, 88, 93–4, 97–102, 105–8, 110, 114, 121, 123, 125–6
Reis, R. 114, 122–3
Republican primary 74–5
Romney, M. 74–6
Rosenblum, N. 125, 127
Rosenthal, H. 102
R packages: LearnBayes 90; MCMCpack 110; Stan 110

Santorum, R. 74–5
Sargent, T. 17

Schickler, E. 73
Shumway, R. and Stoffer, D. 29, 44, 66
signal and noise 5, 9–11, 17, 22–37,
   42–4, 48–66, 74, 92, 94–5, 109,
   120–2, 124
signal-to-noise ratio 9, 25–7, 29–30, 33,
   35, 44, 56–7, 64–6
Simon, H. 94
Sims, C. 122
Skocpol, T. 1
Skowronek, S. 103
Smith, T. 61
Somalia 30
Soroka, S. 83, 90
Spirling, A. 97
Stan, *see* R packages
state-space models 24, 94, 97
Steenbergen, M. 11, 124, 127
Stupak, B. 1
Surowiecki, J. 22
Survey of Professional Forecasters
   114–15
Syria 14

Taber, C. and Lodge, M. 5, 8, 10, 17,
   48–50, 69, 77–8
Taleb, N. 128
time-varying parameter 86, 90, 94, 96,
   102, 104, 109
TIMSS 72

unfavorable news 78, 83–6
updating model 6–8, 14, 16, 42–4, 70,
   75, 77, 79, 89, 109, 113, 116, 121–3,
   125–6

Vietnam War 22, 110
volatility 8, 55–6, 63, 66, 74, 98–9, 101

Watergate 55, 110
Wayne, S. 103
Western, B. and Kleycamp, M. 97
Witko, C. 48
Wlezien, C. 48
Wolfers, J. 114

Zaller, J. 43, 70, 87, 94